Myles Munroe stands as a pillar of strength in the midst of so much windblown confusion that is ripping apart sectors of the Church. His commitment to integrity and spiritual passion—to a biblical lifestyle uncluttered by dead tradition—is a joy to behold.

Jack W. Hayford
Chancellor, The King's College and Seminary
Los Angeles, California

This book will provoke you to fulfill your role of effective and successful leadership.

King for Progress and Development
of the Shai People and State
Ghana, West Africa
(Dr. Kingsley Fletcher)

In this book, Dr. Myles Munroe has identified the soft underbelly of the religious, social, and economic condition of today's world. He has punctured the myths surrounding leadership and leaders and exposed the elusive link for all to see: "Genuine leadership...is an attitude of the heart." Would that this manual invades every library, boardroom, and training centre and conquers the hearts of designated and natural leaders worldwide.

Her Excellency Dame Ivy Dumont
Governor-General
The Commonwealth of The Bahamas

The Spirit of Leadership speaks directly to perhaps one of the greatest needs in our world today....Here is a book laden with profound and practical teachings. When studied and applied, it has the potential to equip millions with the spirit of leadership.

Hon. James Oswald Ingraham, J. P., M. P.
Speaker of the House
The Commonwealth of The Bahamas

THE
SPIRIT
of
LEADERSHIP

THE
SPIRIT
of
LEADERSHIP

DR. MYLES
MUNROE

WHITAKER
HOUSE

THE SPIRIT OF LEADERSHIP

Dr. Myles Munroe
Bahamas Faith Ministries International
P.O. Box N9583
Nassau, Bahamas
e-mail: bfmadmin@bfmmm.com
websites: www.bfmmm.com; www.bfmi.tv; www.mylesmunroe.tv

ISBN-13: 978-0-88368-983-7
ISBN-10: 0-88368-983-9
Printed in the United States of America
© 2005 by Dr. Myles Munroe

WHITAKER
HOUSE
1030 Hunt Valley Circle
New Kensington, PA 15068
www.whitakerhouse.com

Library of Congress Cataloging-in-Publication Data
Munroe, Myles.
The spirit of leadership : cultivating the attitudes that influence human action / Myles Munroe.
p. cm.
Includes bibliographical references.
ISBN 0-88368-983-9 (hardcover : alk. paper)
1. Leadership—Religious aspects—Christianity. 2. Leadership. I. Title.
BV4597.53.L43M86 2004
158'.4—dc22
2004017748

1 2 3 4 5 6 7 8 9 10 11 12 **Ⱳ** 13 12 11 10 09 08 07 06 05

DEDICATION

To my students and all whom I have desired to assist in discovering their true leadership potential.

To all the individuals who have ever quietly dreamt of becoming someone or doing something significant with their lives but could not believe it was possible. To the silent dreamer with a passion for greatness who suffers from the intimidation of his culture and social context.

To the millions of Third World people psychologically trapped under the misconceptions of many misguided would-be leaders who attempted to rob them of their true abilities and leadership potential.

To the aspiring and developing leader within each of us— may we all discover the true meaning of leadership.

To my dear colleagues and fellow trustees of the International Third World Leaders Association. You are truly examples of the spirit of true leadership.

ACKNOWLEDGMENTS

This work is a result of a lifetime of learning and development personally, and it is also the collective contribution of many mentors, teachers, supporters, advisors, friends, and family. I am continually cognizant of the fact that we are all the sum total of what we have learned, as well as the products of the contributions made by so many other people to our lives, as we journey to our ultimate destiny.

No achievement in life is without the help of many known and unknown individuals who have impacted our lives. We owe every measure of our success to the array of input from so many. Here are just a few who made this work possible:

To my beloved wife, Ruth, for your unwavering support.

To my daughter and son, Charissa and Chairo (Myles Jr.), for allowing your dad to pursue his passion and purpose. I love and trust you to manifest the spirit of true leadership.

To Lois Smith Puglisi, my talented and excellent editor. Your relentless pursuit of and patience with me during the inception, development, and delivery of this work was a tremendous source of motivation and encouragement. You're a writer's dream and a gift to the literary arts.

To Bob Whitaker Jr., for your encouragement with this project. You are an asset to the world of publishing.

To the members and followers of BFMI who allowed me the privilege to develop, share, and test the ideas and principles in this book in our relationship over the past twenty-five years. Without you, my vision would have remained just a dream. I am forever grateful.

I also wish to thank the many special friends who encouraged me in this special project, including Willie and Denise Johnson, Her Excellency Dame Ivy Dumont, Governor-General of The Commonwealth of The Islands of The Bahamas, Dr. Lucile Richardson, Dr. Jerry Horner, and my beloved dad, Matthias Munroe.

Finally, I acknowledge and thank the ultimate Leader of all leaders, who himself established the standard for all true leaders to measure up to. I am forever indebted and grateful to you for your eternal gift of life and for igniting within me the spirit of leadership.

CONTENTS

Preface 13

Introduction 18

Part 1: The Leadership Discovery 23

1. The Hidden Leader in You 24

2. What Is a True Leader? 52

3. The Leadership Spirit 81

4. The Spirit of Leadership 123

5. The Loss of the Leadership Spirit 150

6. Leading without Leadership 164

7. The Restoration of the Leadership Spirit 186

8. Leadership Ability without the Attitude 200

9. Recapturing the Spirit of Leadership 208

Part 2: Attitudes of True Leaders 223

10. Purpose and Passion 224

11. Initiative 234

12. Priorities 239

13. Goal Setting 243

14. Teamwork 248

15. Innovation 254

16. Accountability 259

17. Persistence 263

18. Discipline 267

19. Self-Cultivation 271

20. Leadership Attitudes to Cultivate.................... 273

**Appendices: Maximizing
Your Leadership Potential**............................ 279

Essential Qualities and Characteristics
of True Leadership.. 280

Values of the Spirit of Leadership 283

Transforming Followers into Leaders 286

A Word to the Third World 288

Scripture References 290

Notes 296

About the Author.. 299

PREFACE

Trapped within every follower is a hidden leader. The most important quality of true leadership is **the spirit of leadership**. All humans possess the leadership spirit, but only those who capture the spirit of leadership ever become truly effective leaders.

For the past thirty years, I have had the privilege of speaking to hundreds of millions of people through my various media programs and hundreds of thousands personally in my seminars, conferences, and training institutes in over seventy nations. My focus has been assisting others in discovering their sense of purpose, maximizing their untapped potential, and discovering their leadership ability. I have received thousands of testimonies of how the leadership materials, workshops, and seminars have helped many to find their visions, renew their focus, and produce a better life. I am humbled and honored by the privilege of helping others achieve their personal and corporate goals.

A MISSING INGREDIENT

However, there was one challenge that I had for many of these years: I tried to understand why, no matter how many principles, precepts, and programs people were taught on the subject of leadership, there always seemed to be a missing ingredient that was a barrier preventing many of them from breaking through to the leadership capacity that I knew existed within them.

TRAPPED WITHIN EVERY FOLLOWER IS A HIDDEN LEADER.

I had read hundreds of books, articles, journals, and research papers on the subject of leadership; I had attended countless seminars, conferences, and summits dealing with leadership development, yet I was never able to identify, define, or fully understand the mystery key that separated and distinguished the leader from the follower. It was not until a few years ago, during one of my leadership sessions with a group of professionals, business owners, and religious, governmental, and corporate leaders in England that I began to gain insight into this mystery of leadership. I took this insight back to my home in Nassau, Bahamas, where I was able to study my staff and members of our organization to try to clarify specific principles that make a leader different from followers. This book is a result of this study and the subsequent application of these principles in the lives of many of my students and clients.

AN INTERNALIZED DISCOVERY OF SELF

Simply put, I discovered that the **thinking** of a leader is what separates him or her from the followers. I found that true leaders are distinguished by a **unique mental attitude** that emanates from an internalized discovery of self, which creates a strong, positive, and confident self-concept and self-worth. I call this unique mental attitude **the spirit of leadership.** It's an attitude that affects the entire life of the leader and controls his or her response to life, danger, crises, disappointments, failures, challenges, and stress. This attitude gives the leader a sense of confidence, faith, and belief in possibilities. It inspires others to have hope in the face of great odds and causes the leader to cultivate a spirit of purpose, daring, passion, and conviction.

This spirit of leadership is birthed in the womb of a personal revelation within the leader and manifests itself in specific and characteristic qualities. In this book, we will look at how a person can experience his or her personal revelation of leadership, and we will identify the special qualities of this spirit.

LEADERSHIP IS NOT AN EXCLUSIVE CLUB FOR THE ELITE.

Together, we will discover that leadership is not the result of study or ordination, position or power. Man (humanity) is essentially a spirit being, and the nature of a person's spirit dictates the nature that he or she manifests. Until a person's spirit is changed, the person is unchanged. Leadership, therefore, begins in the spirit of a person. When the spirit of leadership comes alive, it produces an attitude that separates the leader from the follower.

It is important to understand that leadership is not an exclusive club for the elite few who were "born with it." **Every human has the instinct and capacity for leadership, but most do not have the courage or will to cultivate it.** The spirit called "man" was created to lead, but man lost the spirit of leadership. All humans posses the potential to lead, but most have lost the passion of leadership. The goal of this book is to help you to rediscover and recover that leadership spirit.

There are many who confuse the position of leadership with the disposition of true leadership. No matter what position one may be given, status in an organization does not automatically create leadership. **Genuine leadership is one's internal disposition, which relates to a sense of purpose, self-worth, and self-concept.**

Others have confused leadership with the ability to control others through manipulating their emotions and playing on their fears and needs. **But true leadership is a product of inspiration, not manipulation.**

Then there are those who believe that the title makes the leader. However, we have all seen many people who have been placed in prominent positions with impressive titles yet have failed miserably because they haven't understood that real leadership is manifested in performance and results and not just in labels.

True leadership goes far beyond the mechanics of most of the approaches that pervade our leadership programs today. It has more to do with discovering a sense of meaning and significance in life. This distinction separates the leadership quality of passion from the hunger or lust for power. **True leaders do not seek power but are driven by a passion to achieve a noble cause.**

I am convinced that you were created to be a leading success. Every human being was created to lead in an area of gifting. You were never created to be oppressed, subjugated, subordinated, or depressed. The Creator designed each human being to fulfill a specific purpose and assignment in life. Your assignment determines your area of leadership. Deep inside each of us is a spirit with a big dream struggling to free itself from the limitations of our past experiences, present circumstances, and self-imposed doubts.

We are all victims of unfulfilled passions. I believe that man's greatest ignorance is of himself. What you believe about yourself creates your world. No human can live beyond the limits of his or her beliefs. In essence, you are what you believe: **Your beliefs are a product of your thoughts, your thoughts create your beliefs, your beliefs create your convictions, your convictions create your attitude, your attitude controls your perception, and your perception dictates your behavior.** The result is that your life is what you *think* it should be. When you think according to the spirit of leadership, you begin the process of becoming a leader. This is the heart of true leadership: your attitude, your mind-set, your "spirit of the mind."

Some of the unique attitudes or qualities of leaders include passion, initiative, teamwork, innovation, persistence, discipline, focus, time management, confidence, positive disposition, patience, peace, and compassion. We will explore many of these leadership attitudes so that you can discover how to cultivate them in your life.

This book is dedicated to helping you recapture the essence of your true leadership potential and the accompanying mental attitude that will manifest the **true spirit of leadership.**

INTRODUCTION

Leadership is a trusted privilege given by followers.

T here is nothing as elusive as leadership. **All the money in the world can make you rich, and all the power in the world can make you strong, but these things can never make you a leader.** You can inherit a fortune but never leadership. Yet there is no greater need in our twenty-first century world than effective, competent leadership. Our greatest challenge is that of a leadership vacuum. The number one need all over the globe today is not money, social programs, or even new governments. It is quality, moral, disciplined, principle-centered leadership.

We need true leadership in our governments, businesses, schools, civic institutions, youth communities, religious organizations, homes, and in every arena of life—including the disciplines of law, medicine, science, sports, and the media. Yet the search for genuine leadership is becoming more difficult.

WHERE ARE THE TRUE LEADERS?

The complex, uncertain, uncharted waters of the twenty-first century have plunged us in to a world of globalization, terrorism, economic uncertainty, famines, health epidemics, social transformation, corporate compromises, moral and ethical experimentation, religious conflicts, and cultural clashes. These conditions demand the highest quality of leadership that our generation can produce. Yet I have sat in the halls of governments and observed the struggles of today's leaders. I have sat around the table chatting with presidents of countries, and I have heard them express their lack of ability to deal with their nations' challenges. I have talked with cabinet ministers of governments around the world, and they openly ask for help, assistance, and advice. Many leaders just don't know how to lead any longer.

THERE IS NOTHING AS ELUSIVE AS LEADERSHIP.

This crisis in leadership is on many people's minds today. Questions of moral integrity, honor, values, role models, and respectable standards are topics of discussion on many news programs, and they are also in the thoughts of the man on the street. We hear of leaders having sexual escapades. We hear of business magnates falling by the dozens to corruption. We see national leaders and their cabinet members being tried by their own governments for stealing and other financial misconduct. We learn of priests abusing and misusing their authority and positions in order to take advantage of those whom they were entrusted to care for. *Where are the true leaders today?*

I believe the problem is that leadership has become a role one plays rather than a life one leads. Contemporary leaders are attempting to divorce their personal lives from their public responsibilities and their personal standards from their public lives. To many, leadership is an act, not a calling. Therefore, when they are in their offices, they act a certain way, but when they leave, they lead double lives. This is a contradiction of true leadership. Leadership is not a technique, a style, or the acquisition of skills, but a manifestation of a spirit.

Many institutions, Fortune 500 companies, government agencies, civic organizations, and nonprofit entities spend billions of dollars every year training thousands of would-be leaders in management techniques, human manipulation skills, organizational systems, methods of control and persuasion, and much more, in the hopes of producing potential or better leaders. Yet such seminars cannot produce true leaders. Furthermore, the quality and standards of leaders are not increasing, but decreasing.

LEADERSHIP HAS BECOME A ROLE ONE PLAYS RATHER THAN A LIFE ONE LEADS.

The shelves of every bookstore are stacked with books on the subject of leadership. Some promise instant transformation from follower to leader, while others sell cheap ideas that purport to create leaders by the application of shallow psychology and worn-out principles that frustrate those who invest in them. Research on how to be a leader continues by the leadership gurus, as colleges and universities add special courses designed to produce or improve the cadre of leaders. Yet I believe that all the college courses in leadership can never make a leader.

Many of those whom we idolized as leaders in our modern societies have disappointed us as their fragile, formerly hidden inconsistencies have been exposed. Just the mention of Enron, WorldCom, Tyco, Martha Stewart, Richard Nixon, Bill Clinton, and Catholic priests tells the story of our culture of defective leadership. Moral defects; abuses of power, privilege, and trust; misuses of resources; corruption; and hypocrisy have become associated with leadership today perhaps more than at any other time in history.

Morality, ethics, principles, convictions, standards, faithfulness, transparency, trustworthiness, and honesty are rare commodities in the field of contemporary leadership. Why is true leadership so difficult to find?

OUR CHEATING CULTURE OF LEADERSHIP

One day, as I settled in to my seat on a plane trip to address a group of leaders on ethics and morality in leadership, I was shocked to discover, in the copy of the *American Way* magazine in my seat pocket, an article by Joseph Guinto with this title: "Lie, Cheat, and Steal Your Way to the Top." The subtitle read, "Everyone's doing it, right? But what's our cheating culture really costing us, and where and when does it end?" Obviously, this subject caught my eye, and I plunged into reading the content.

The article exposed and detailed the corrupting web of cheating as a culture at all levels of Western society, including the highest offices of leadership, and it talked about the "trickle-down corruption effect" taking place. Here are some facts contained in the article that I think are noteworthy: "Employee theft is one of the fastest-growing crimes in the U.S.A....the total cost of occupational fraud—mainly accounting schemes—was $600 billion in 2002...twice what it was in 1997." The article said that one of the results of this widespread corruption is its effect on the mind-set of future business leaders. An ethics professor at a top business school said, "[My] students defend their view that some cheating is okay by saying, 'Everybody does it.'"[1]

WE ARE IN NEED OF TRUE, SPIRITUALLY CONSCIOUS LEADERS.

This is the culture and environment of leadership that pervades our world today, whether it is in politics, religion, business, education, or sports. We are in desperate need of true, competent, principled, sensitive, compassionate, and spiritually conscious leaders.

WHAT MAKES A TRUE LEADER?

What makes a leader? How are genuine leaders produced? When does one truly become a leader? Is there a predictor of leadership? What are the qualities that distinguish leaders from followers? This book is about the missing ingredient in leadership development. It's about the elusive link between talent, titles, and leadership. Genuine leadership is not a result of memorizing formulas, learning skills, imitating methods, or training in techniques. It is an attitude of the heart.

PART ONE:
THE LEADERSHIP DISCOVERY

CHAPTER ONE
THE HIDDEN LEADER IN YOU

Trapped within every follower is an undiscovered leader.

An army of sheep led by a lion will always defeat an army of lions led by a sheep. This statement captures the spirit of this book. This concept became real to me during one of my trips to the continent of the cradle of humanity, Africa. It was there, deep in the village lands of the African bush, that I heard a story that encapsulated what I have come to understand as the missing link in the leadership development process.

It was a sunny but cool day in the bustling, modern city of Harare, the capital of the southern African nation of Zimbabwe. I had just finished speaking in the conference center of the Harare Hilton to over 5,000 leaders. As the guest of one of the largest community organizations in the nation, I had been invited to provide leadership training and motivational sessions for aspiring and seasoned leaders. This was our last session after over seven days of presentations. At the end of the session, my host asked if I would consider going to another town to speak to an additional group of leaders who had asked if I would come to them.

I gladly consented, and arrangements were made for my driver—who also served as my interpreter—and me to leave at first light the next morning.

We started out at six o'clock, and after driving for almost two hours, we finally left the modern city lights and were greeted by unpaved roads, dusty villages, and dense green forests. Just when I thought we were about to arrive, my driver indicated that we still had another two hours to go before we arrived at our village destination. Suddenly, I realized that we were headed for a safari experience. After another bumpy two hours through what seemed to be jungle, we finally entered a clearing. There stood a group of children who suddenly broke into wild, excited chanting, as if they had just experienced the end of a long anticipation.

AN ARMY OF SHEEP LED BY A LION WILL ALWAYS DEFEAT AN ARMY OF LIONS LED BY A SHEEP.

As we came to a noisy stop, a group of happy men emerged from a large thatched hut. They were led by a gentle man wearing a welcoming smile and simple clothing. We embraced, and he invited me in to the grass-roofed building in which over three hundred men and women sat eagerly waiting for us to begin the teaching session. I was deeply humbled by the hunger and patience of these beautiful people, and I gave them my best. It was a joy to be so well received.

After the session, the chief of the village invited me to a special dinner in my honor where I was treated to cuisines traditional to village life and culture—some familiar to me and some not. It was during this meal that the chief told me the story that taught me a lesson in leadership I will never forget.

A LION AMONG SHEEP

There was once a farmer who lived in this village and also was a herder of sheep. One day, he took his sheep out to pasture, and while they were grazing, he suddenly heard a strange noise coming from a patch of grass, which first sounded like a kitten. Led by his curiosity, the old shepherd went to see what was the source of this insistent sound, and to his surprise, he found a lone shivering lion cub, obviously separated from his family. His first thought was the danger he would be in if he stayed too close to the cub and his parents returned. So the old man quickly left the area and watched from a distance to see if the mother lion or the pack would return. However, after the sun began to set, and there was still no activity to secure the lion cub, the shepherd decided that, in his best judgment, and for the safety and survival of the lion cub, he would take him to his farmhouse and care for him.

THE LION HAD BECOME A SHEEP BY ASSOCIATION.

Over the next eight months, the shepherd hand-fed this cub with fresh milk and kept him warm, safe, and secure in the protective confines of the farmhouse. After the cub had grown into a playful, energetic ball of shiny muscle, he would take him out daily with the sheep to graze. The lion cub grew with the sheep and became a part of the herd. They accepted him as one of their own, and he acted like one of them. After fifteen months had passed, the little cub had become an adolescent lion, but he acted, sounded, responded, and behaved just like one of the sheep. In essence, the lion had become a sheep by association. He had lost himself and become one of them.

One hot day, four years later, the shepherd sat on a rock, taking refuge in the slight shade of a leafless tree. He watched over his flock as they waded into the quiet, flowing water of a river to drink. The lion who thought he was a sheep followed them in to the water to drink. Suddenly, just across the river, there appeared out of the thick jungle bush a large beast that the lion cub had never seen before. The sheep panicked and, as if under the spell of some survival instinct, leaped out of the water and dashed toward the direction of the farm. They never stopped until they were all safely huddled behind the fence of the pen. Strangely, the lion cub, who was now a grown lion, was also huddled with them, stricken with fear.

While the flock scrambled for the safety of the farm, the beast made a sound that seemed to shake the forest. When he lifted his head above the tall grass, the shepherd could see that he held in his blood-drenched mouth the lifeless body of a lamb from the flock. The man knew that danger had returned to his part of the forest.

Seven days passed without further incident, and then, while the flock grazed, the young lion went down to the river to drink. As he bent over the water, he suddenly panicked and ran wildly toward the farmhouse for safety. The sheep did not run and wondered why he had, while the lion wondered why the sheep had not run since he had seen the beast again. After a while, the young lion went slowly back to the flock and then to the water to drink again. Once more, he saw the beast and froze in panic. It was his own reflection in the water.

While he tried to understand what he was seeing, suddenly, the beast appeared out of the jungle again. The flock dashed with breakneck speed toward the farmhouse, but before the young lion could move, the beast stepped in the water toward him and made that deafening sound that filled the forest. For a moment, the young lion felt that his life was about to end. He realized that he saw not just one beast, but two—one in the water and one before him.

His head was spinning with confusion as the beast came within ten feet of him and growled at him face-to-face with frightening power in a way that seemed to say to him, "Try it, and come and follow me."

HE FELT STIRRINGS THAT HE HAD NEVER KNOWN BEFORE.

As fear gripped the young lion, he decided to try to appease the beast and make the same sound. However, the only noise that came from his gaping jaws was the sound of a sheep. The beast responded with an even louder burst that seemed to say, "Try it again." After seven or eight attempts, the young lion suddenly heard himself make the same sound as the beast. He also felt stirrings in his body and feelings that he had never known before. It was as if he was experiencing a total transformation in mind, body, and spirit.

Suddenly, there stood in the river of life two beasts growling at and to each other. Then the shepherd saw something he would never forget. As the beastly sounds filled the forest for miles around, the big beast stopped, turned his back on the young lion, and started toward the forest. Then he paused and looked at the young lion one more time and growled, as if to say, "Are you coming?" The young lion knew what the gesture meant and suddenly realized that his day of decision had arrived—the day he would have to choose whether to continue to live life as a sheep or to be the self he had just discovered. He knew that, to become his true self, he would have to give up the safe, secure, predictable, and simple life of the farm and enter the frightening, wild, untamed, unpredictable, dangerous life of the jungle. It was a day to become true to himself and leave the false image of another life behind. It was an invitation to a "sheep" to become the king of the jungle. Most importantly, it was an invitation for the body of a lion to possess the spirit of a lion.

After looking back and forth at the farm and the jungle a few times, the young lion turned his back on the farm and the sheep with whom he had lived for years, and he followed the beast into the forest to become who he always had been—a lion king.

LASTING CHANGE CAN OCCUR ONLY WHEN IT TAKES PLACE IN THE SPIRIT OF THE MIND.

As I sat there listening to this fantastic story, I was engulfed by the revelation of the deep principles it communicated relating to leaders, leadership, and the critical process involved in discovering and becoming your true self. I went away from that village with a deeper understanding of why it is so difficult for many individuals to make that transition across the river to their true selves. I suddenly understood that lasting change could occur only when it took place in the spirit of the mind. Without this metamorphosis, no amount of training, study, or education could transform a follower into a leader. In essence, a converted attitude is the key to a transformed life. Until this attitude change happens, the lion will still think, act, respond, and live like a sheep instead of the king of the jungle.

A DECISION AFFECTING THE FUTURE

Just as the young lion's genuine growl revealed his inherent strength, you can release the inherent leadership strength within you when you come to understand your true self. Just as the young lion watched the beast walking away and knew that he had to make a decision about his future, you have a choice to make about your own future.

Just as the young lion looked back at the farm where the sheep were and then looked toward the forest where the lion was heading, you have to evaluate your past and your potential and step toward one or the other. Just as the young lion knew that, to become his true self, he would have to give up the safe, secure, predictable, and simple life of the farm and enter the frightening, wild, untamed, unpredictable, dangerous life of the jungle, you will have to leave the safe confines of being a follower if you are going to become a leader.

Just as the young lion turned his back on the farm, crossed the river, and walked into the forest—leaving behind his old life as a sheep and embarking on the life he was born to live—so this book is designed to challenge you to cross your own river of intimidation and fear and enter the forest of the spirit of leadership, which you were created to manifest.

As one who has had to cross that river myself, my desire is to be a catalyst, like the beast, roaring an invitation into your life and heart and hopefully helping you to enter the adventure of discovering and releasing the leadership spirit within you.

THE POWER OF ATTITUDE

There is nothing as powerful as attitude. Attitude dictates your response to the present and determines the quality of your future. You are your attitude, and your attitude is you. If you do not control your attitude, it will control you.

Attitude creates your world and designs your destiny. It determines your success or failure in any venture in life. More opportunities have been lost, withheld, and forfeited because of attitude than from any other cause. Attitude is a more powerful distinction in life than beauty, power, title, or social status. It is more important than wealth—and it can keep one poor. It is the servant that can open the doors of life or close the gates of possibility. It can make beauty ugly and homeliness attractive. The distinguishing factor between a winner or a loser is attitude. The difference between a leader and a follower is attitude.

> ## ATTITUDE CREATES YOUR WORLD AND DESIGNS YOUR DESTINY.

What is attitude? We will discuss this topic in detail in coming chapters, but for now let me simply define attitude as "the mind-set or mental conditioning that determines our interpretation of and response to our environments." It's our way of thinking. It is also important to understand that attitude is a natural product of the integration of our self-worth, self-concepts, self-esteem, and sense of value or significance. In essence, your attitude is the manifestation of who you think you are. **Leaders think differently**

about themselves, and this distinguishes them from followers.

The story of the lion and the sheep demonstrates the power of attitude. We live our attitudes and our attitudes create our lives. The difference between the attitudes of a lion and a sheep determines their place in the scheme of the animal kingdom. Perhaps that is why the Creator, as recorded in the books of the Hebrew writer Moses and other biblical writers, identifies himself with the unique temperaments or natures of certain animals.

We live our lives based on who we think we are. According to the illustration, if you believe in your heart that you are a sheep, then you will stay in the confines that others have placed you in or that you have made for yourself. If you think that you are a lion, then you will venture beyond manmade limitations and embark on the life of leadership that you were born to live. You will develop into someone who inspires and influences others within your inherent domain.

No amount of training in leadership skills, courses in management methods, power titles, promotions, or associations can substitute for the right attitudes. I am convinced that all the money in the world may make you rich, but it can never make you a leader. Your leadership development is determined by your perceptions of who you are and why you exist—in other words, your sense of significance to life.

DESIGNED TO LEAD OUR ENVIRONMENTS

This point is fundamental to understanding our leadership potential and capacity as humans. Therefore, let me offer you a somewhat technical definition of our reason for living. It is my firm belief that the nature of each human being is to be in control of his environment and circumstances. **Each of us was created to rule, govern, control, master, manage, and lead our environments. You are in essence a leader, no matter who you are,** regardless of whether you manifest it or not. Whether you are rich, poor, young, old, male, female, black, white, a citizen of an industrialized nation, a citizen of a third-world nation, educated, or uneducated—you have the nature and capacity for leadership. Yet you can fulfill your inherent leadership potential only when you discover, understand, develop, and begin to exercise who you are designed to be and the nature of your true leadership potential.

No MATTER WHO YOU ARE, YOU HAVE THE NATURE AND CAPACITY FOR LEADERSHIP.

It doesn't matter whether you are the CEO of a large corporation, a teacher, a homemaker, the owner of a small business, a construction worker, an artist, a clerk, a government worker, a farmer, a student, a doctor, or any other vocation or position in life: **The self-discovery of your inherent leadership potential and an understanding of who you are and what you are meant to be are the keys to fulfilling your purpose for existence as a leader.**

Title, position, power, notoriety, fame, or family name cannot make you a true leader. For example, you can hire someone as a manager in a company. You can give him a title, a budget, a desk, a staff, and everything else. But then suppose he doesn't take initiative. He doesn't try to solve problems by himself, seek better ways of performing tasks or improving systems, or understand that part of management is pushing the boundaries and exploring new concepts and ideas. He just does as he's told and doesn't disturb policy or challenge old, outdated methods. That's not leadership.

In essence, there are some unique attitudes of leaders that distinguish them from followers, and these attitudes produce certain behaviors that stretch the leader beyond the limitations of the norm. It is these attitudes that we will explore and call the "spirit of leadership." Therefore, being in the position of a follower doesn't negate your inherent leadership potential. Knowing and cultivating certain attitudes about yourself will give you the mind-set you need to develop your leadership potential to the fullest and fulfill what you were born to do.

A NATURAL INSTINCT FOR LEADERSHIP

Though we often don't recognize it for what it is, every human on this planet has a natural inclination for leadership, in one form or another. As birds have an instinct to fly and fish have an instinct to swim, humans have an instinct to be in control of their lives, circumstances, decisions, or environments. When we aren't in control, we want to be.

Perhaps this is why the natural human instinct or response is frustration, depression, discomfort, or even psychological and physical illness when we are under the control of creditors, banking institutions, or even friends to whom we have obligations. It is because our circumstances are dominating us, and our spiritual, psychological, and physical natures were not designed to live under these conditions.

We were not designed to be dominated. When we are not in charge of our lives, we feel bound and restricted. For example, if you have a thirty-year mortgage on your home, you don't feel free until you pay it off. Even though you're enjoying your house, there's a voice in the back of your mind saying, "But it's still theirs. It belongs to them for as long as they've got that paper."

On the other hand, why do you experience relief and contentment when all your bills are paid? When you get a bonus and it covers all your debts and you don't owe anyone anything, all of a sudden, you get a smile on your face. You want to say hello to everybody you meet. Am I right? When all your needs are met, you feel as if you're walking on top of the world. That's because you are experiencing what you were born for. You were designed to be able to manage your environment.

YOU WERE DESIGNED TO BE ABLE TO MANAGE YOUR ENVIRONMENT.

Many people want to make a lot of money, but it's usually not because they want the money itself. The fundamental desire for wealth is motivated by the desire for power—power to dominate and control lifestyle, circumstances, and environment. It's the power that money gives us that makes us pursue it. Every human naturally wants to control his life, and money or wealth seems to promise this power of control. We are after the feeling or sense of dominion that we get from the ability to buy what we want, live where we wish, eat what we desire, wear what we fancy, and go wherever we decide to. It is the power over circumstances and, in some cases, over people, that we seek.

This desire to have control over our lives explains many of the problems in our world. For instance, why does a young teenage boy get a gun, walk in to a store, and say, "Everybody hit the ground!" Imagine that you're in the middle of such a situation. Suppose that the boy is thirteen years old and you're thirty-four; he's 5 feet tall, and you're 6 feet. You know that you're physically stronger than he is. But since he has the advantage of a dangerous weapon that threatens your life, you have to cooperate with his commands. For one brief moment, that young man feels what he was born to feel—what is called a "rush." It is a strange sense of power, control, and invincibility.

Our society puts a young man like this in a juvenile detention center, and he does his time and comes back out. But he *remembers that feeling* and is haunted by the temptation to repeat the act. I believe that this is more than a psychological issue. It involves that deep spiritual desire in the nature of man to dominate his environment. It's tied to how he feels about himself. I'm convinced that the desire for power over others is a distortion of something good; it's a distortion of our inherent human desire to exercise leadership dominion.

LEADERSHIP AND OUR BELIEFS ABOUT ORIGIN

Where do most of our attitudes about leadership come from? Whether you think you are a leader or not, your ideas about leadership are probably a conditioned response.

Generally, we have been taught that leadership is reserved for an exclusive group of people who were handpicked by destiny to control, rule, and subordinate the masses. I want to demonstrate to you that, contrary to popular opinion, **leadership is not an elite club for a certain few. It is the true essence of all human beings.**

GENERALLY, OUR IDEAS ABOUT LEADERSHIP ARE CONDITIONED RESPONSES.

I have found that people's concepts of their origin often influence the way they think about themselves, including their ideas about their leadership potential. In our world, there are two major theories about origin: evolution and creation. There are several variations to evolutionary theory, but many evolutionists believe that the universe was formed as a result of an explosion of energy. This is known as the big bang theory. Over millions of years, microscopic life developed on earth, out of which came animal species that mutated, with the stronger species winning out over the weaker ones in a survival of the fittest. At this point in our history, human beings are the most advanced of the species.

According to this theory, humans are, at their essence, sophisticated amoebas. There is no specific purpose for life—it exists merely as a result of forces of nature. This theory also supports the idea that those who are stronger—physically, intellectually, or creatively—are destined to lead and control others, while the rest are destined to be followers.

The other major theory of humanity's origin is creation. This is the idea that an intelligent Being formed the universe and created the earth, the vegetation, the animals, and human beings. Some creationists believe that the Creator made the world and then left it to its own devices, while others believe that the Architect of the earth is still actively involved in it and made humanity with a specific nature and purpose. This concept supports the idea that every person has a role and contribution to make, no matter what their station in life and current level of ability.

WE ARE THE PRODUCTS OF A HIGHLY INTELLIGENT AND CREATIVE SUPREME BEING.

Evolution is still a theory. It has not been proven. There is no hard evidence to verify its claims. It's a very interesting premise, yet I believe that the experience and makeup of the human creature defies the evolutionary concept. The intricate design of human beings and the orderly nature of the universe don't support it.

The alternative is that there must have been a higher, more sophisticated creative process than the arbitrary process of evolution. The ancient writings, as recorded in the first book written by Moses, present a more plausible and reasonable explanation of our origins: We are the products of a highly intelligent and creative Supreme Being. The proposition in the first two chapters of Genesis is that God personally and purposefully created human beings in his own image and likeness and then told them to be fruitful, fill the earth, and rule over it. They were to be stewards of the earth, responsible for its care and well-being. We should note that the Creator designed human beings in his image and likeness *after* he made the vegetation and the animals, specifically separating them from the rest of creation in some important ways.

The ancient account says that he brought the rest of creation into being with statements such as "Let there be light" or "Let the land produce living creatures." Yet when it came to one particular creature, he said, "Let *us* make man *in our image, in our likeness*." Human beings were the only creatures who were indicated as being made in the image and likeness of their Creator. This means that they have his nature. A significant aspect of that nature is the ability to plan ahead, imagine, create, and effectively administer the manifestation of plans. In other words, being made in his image means having the nature or spirit of leadership.

The Origin of Our Leadership Spirit

The Creator poured out his own nature into human beings when he established their nature, and this is the origin of our leadership spirit. In this sense, we are a portion of the poured-out God. As the Creator is purposeful, organizational, and creative, we are designed to be the same.

You have to decide which concept of origin you will accept as the basis for your life. Only you can choose what you believe about yourself and human nature, as well as the nature of leadership. Is leadership only for the strong who are able to win out over the weak, or perhaps only for those who receive it by fate? Or is leadership an inherent part of our design as human beings? My experience and observations of humanity support the latter belief and are the basis for what I describe in the rest of this book as our human vocation.

I believe that you and I were created to lead. **Leadership is inherent in our nature and is fundamental to our origins, our human makeup—and our destiny.**

MYTHS ABOUT LEADERSHIP

Partly because our contemporary society has accepted a "survival of the fittest" mind-set, many of us have come to believe certain myths about leadership. These ideas have been fostered by our families, cultures, and nations. In addition, much of the theoretical foundations for our beliefs about leadership are derived from the thoughts of great Greek philosophers, such as Plato, Aristotle, and Socrates.

OUR PHILOSOPHIES DETERMINE THE WAY WE THINK.

During the height of the golden age of the Hellenistic period, the art of human nature, social development, the control and management of the masses, and the study of governmental structures for national development were the subject of great debate and research. The art of leadership was among the principal subjects studied and discussed, and the conclusions were so potent that most of our present-day beliefs, philosophy, and concepts of leadership and governing can be traced back to the ideas of these philosophers.

This issue is vitally important because our beliefs, convictions, and ideas form our personal philosophies and serve as the source of our perceptions of ourselves and others, as well as of life itself. In essence, our philosophies determine the way we think. In fact, **we live our thoughts and manifest them in our attitudes toward ourselves and others. We cannot live beyond our thoughts and convictions.**

It is my belief that many of our current theories of leadership have produced a number of myths that must be understood, studied, and challenged. Many leadership "gurus" have identified and articulated these myths. They can be summarized as follows:

MYTH #1
BIRTH TRAIT THEORY:
"LEADERS ARE BORN, NOT MADE."

This theory is the belief that leadership is a result of special birth traits inherent in the personality and nature of the individual. It implies that some humans are born with unique qualities that earmark them for leadership, while the others—the majority, who do not possess these traits—are destined to be led.

WE CANNOT LIVE BEYOND OUR THOUGHTS AND CONVICTIONS.

This concept leads us to deify our leaders as men and women who are essentially unlike us and therefore superior to us. This philosophy results in our blocking our own leadership potential and development and surrendering our untapped leadership capacity to the control and limitations of others. When this happens on a cultural level, we can even stunt the growth of our countries' next generation of leaders.

MYTH #2:
LEADERSHIP BY PROVIDENCE

There is a belief that certain people are chosen by "the gods" and appointed to the elite position of leadership over the unfortunate masses. In essence, leadership is reserved for the few chosen by a divine power to control, manage, and direct the life, future, fortunes, and aspirations of the un-chosen.

MYTH #3
*LEADERSHIP IS THE RESULT OF
A CHARISMATIC PERSONALITY*

This is the theory that only certain individuals who possess a unique measure of charisma; who exhibit special traits, such as a force of will; who are extroverts; who are magnetic speakers, and so on, are leaders. The difficulty with this theory is that, in every generation, there arise significant leaders who do not display the charismatic traits celebrated by this philosophy.

In many cases, leaders emerge from the unique circumstances of the times in which they live without manifesting any special charisma. Sometimes, it takes a crisis for someone to step forward and reveal his or her leadership ability. Certain people's past or present status as leaders should not keep us from acknowledging that other people—including ourselves—are potential leaders in particular spheres or circumstances of life.

MYTH #4
*LEADERSHIP IS THE PRODUCT OF
A FORCEFUL PERSONALITY*

This theory emerges from the belief that leadership is the result of an authoritarian, coldly calculating, no-nonsense, hard-driving, impatient, quick-tempered, and moody personality. This false perception comes from the idea that people are fundamentally incompetent and naturally lazy and have to be forced, threatened, and manipulated by their leaders and managers if anything is going to be accomplished. However, the evidence has always defied this belief, showing that people are most productive and cooperative when they are inspired rather than manipulated by leadership.

MYTH #5
LEADERSHIP IS THE RESULT OF SPECIAL TRAINING

This is the belief that leaders are produced through special educational courses and training. Many people feel that they have to have an MBA or attend leadership conferences in order to be able to lead others. There's nothing wrong with such training, in itself. Yet as I wrote in the Introduction, true leadership is not a technique, a method, a style, or the acquisition of skills. It is the manifestation of an attitude based on the knowledge of who you were born to be. Your attitude about yourself has a tremendous impact on your daily life and whether you fulfill your central life purpose.

WE SHOULD NEVER LET ANYBODY GET THE IDEA THAT WE DON'T HAVE WILLS OF OUR OWN.

We have allowed circumstances, other people, and our own unsubstantiated beliefs to block our natural leadership tendencies. We should never allow anybody to get the idea that we don't have a will or some sense of point of view or unique perspective of our own. Others may be in positions of authority over us, which we should respect, but that doesn't mean that they should stifle our inherent potential as leaders.

In this book, I will introduce an alternative philosophy of leadership that challenges the above theories and traditional concepts of leadership potential. I call this theory the "inherent nature of leadership."

IT'S ALL ABOUT ATTITUDE

The essence of leadership, again, is not in techniques for controlling and manipulating people, which seem to be popular in leadership training today. All the college courses in business administration you may take, all the leadership methods you learn, and all the management seminars you attend can give you information, but they cannot develop you into a real leader.

THE ESSENCE OF LEADERSHIP IS NOT IN TECHNIQUES; IT'S IN OUR ATTITUDES.

True leadership is an attitude that naturally inspires and motivates others, and it comes from an internalized discovery about yourself. You cannot "learn" an attitude. If someone learns an attitude, it's called conditioning or mere mental assent. That's not leadership.

You can condition an animal to do something by rewarding or threatening it with an external result. But an attitude is a perspective, a motivation, or a desire that comes from within and is not based on a temporary external consequence. It is something deeply personal and internal that influences and transforms your thinking about yourself and your ability, value, self-worth, self-esteem, outlook on life, actions, and perceptions of others.

"AS YOU THINK, SO SHALL YOU BE"

Learning about leadership and knowing what it means to be a leader are two different things. **Learning comes from education, while knowing comes from revelation. Learning is cognitive, while knowing is spiritual.** You do not really change until you "know." Knowing changes your mind, which transforms your attitude, which, in turn, informs, directs, and regulates your behavior.

William James wrote, "The greatest discovery of our generation is that human beings can alter their lives by altering their attitudes of mind. As you think, so shall you be."[2] This was really a rediscovery because, centuries earlier, another generation heard a similar truth from King Solomon, the wisest and richest man of his day, who essentially said, "As a man thinks in his heart, so is he." What a person thinks in his heart is what will ultimately come out in his actions. However, the challenge is in knowing how to change one's attitude. If attitude transformation were simple, then many of us would have changed a number of times during our lifetimes.

Most of us are not leaders today because, in our hearts, we don't believe that is who we are. From my extensive experience in training people in leadership, I have found that what is often missing is a sense of the inherent leadership spirit that lies within them. What and how we think about our purpose in the world is the basis of our attitudes and actions, toward others and ourselves.

Your future and ability to succeed aren't tied to what others think of you. They are tied to what you think of yourself. The source of your attitude is your mind-set and thoughts. That's really what the spirit of leadership is all about.

THE LEADERSHIP SPIRIT AND THE SPIRIT OF LEADERSHIP

In this book, I make a distinction between the leadership spirit and the spirit of leadership so that you can better understand your leadership potential and the attitude that accompanies it. We were given the leadership spirit when we were created. Our leadership potential is still intact, but we have lost the spirit of leadership—that is, the consciousness of our being made in the image of our Creator, as well as the attitudes that accompany that awareness, which are the foundation of true leadership.

We still have the raw material of leadership potential, but most of us don't have the desire, courage, or will to use it as we are meant to. It's like planting a fertile field but not having any rain to make the grain grow. Or it's like owning a Rolls-Royce but not having any gasoline to run it. You possess something with powerful promise, but you are unable to maximize its full potential. In essence, we possess the aptitude, but we lack the attitude that activates this untapped power. We've been emptied of the Spirit that is meant to empower us for living and enable us to be what we were intended to be. Some people have, instinctively or purposefully, been able to tap into their leadership ability, as we will see in the next chapter, but most of us have not.

ATTITUDE CREATES ENVIRONMENT

We must have a clear understanding that true leadership is an attitude of the heart birthed by a renewed understanding of purpose. It is more a matter of being something than doing something. It is a self-discovery that translates into meaningful activities such as creating, building, and nurturing.

This brings us back to our inherent human desire to be in control of our circumstances. **Because true leaders discover and understand who they are and what their purpose is, they influence their environments more than their environments influence them.** Have you noticed how, when some people find themselves in financial difficulty, they immediately start finding and working on solutions to the problem, while other people panic, lose hope, surrender to their circumstances, and become immobilized by the debt? Do you know people who can turn a one-room apartment into a beautiful and comfortable haven that is more appealing and inviting than many mansions?

TRUE LEADERS INFLUENCE THEIR ENVIRONMENTS MORE THAN THEIR ENVIRONMENTS INFLUENCE THEM.

These simple examples show different ways in which people tap in to their leadership abilities and influence their environments rather than the other way around. There are innumerable applications of this principle in everyday life, on both large and small scales, depending on people's gifts and calling. True leaders strive to overcome crises, and they become creative in difficulty.

CAPTURE AND CULTIVATE THE SPIRIT OF LEADERSHIP

All of us must capture and cultivate the spirit of leadership, this attitude of shaping and forming our lives according to our purposes. **Though every human being on this planet has an inclination for leadership, most of us do not have the courage to cultivate it.** This is a very serious problem. We've been so conditioned by discouragement, failure, or the oppression of others that we are afraid to follow our natural leadership instincts. We make excuses, such as "I'm too shy," "I'm not as gifted as he is," "I don't have the education," "My family was never good at that," and so on.

Relatively few people in the entire human race ever capture or discover the spirit of leadership to the point where they ignite their leadership potential. Our challenge is to nurture our leadership instincts to the extent that we can rise from being followers to being leaders in our inherent domains.

YOU WERE BORN TO LEAD, BUT YOU MUST BECOME A LEADER.

When you make the decision to cultivate your intrinsic leadership potential, a transition will occur. You will become like the young lion who left the sheep pen and went into the forest so that he could fulfill his true nature. Did he face the uncertainty, challenges, and danger of the forest? Yes. But he also became what he was designed to be. He learned, grew, and became a leader by discovering the potential within himself.

DISCOVER THE LEADER WITHIN YOU

The leadership potential within you is waiting to be discovered. This book will enable you to identify the nature and attitudes that correspond to the leadership spirit so that you can become all that you were designed to be.

Again, true leadership is self-discovery. It has very little to do with what you *do,* but is fundamentally a matter of becoming who you *are.* It is the result of one's commitment to self-manifestation.

You were *born* to lead, but you must *become* a leader. Every human being was endowed by the Creator with leadership potential in a specific area of gifting. The human spirit is designed to manage and control its world, and it functions best when creating an environment conducive to this pursuit.

You are a leader, regardless of your present status or your feelings about your leadership ability and potential. When you discover this truth and become convinced of it, then you won't be content with just being a follower any longer. You will learn the secret to becoming a leader by discovering the hidden leader within.

Are you ready to step out and embark on the life you were born to live?

CHAPTER PRINCIPLES

1. Trapped within every follower is an undiscovered leader.

2. An army of sheep led by a lion will always defeat an army of lions led by a sheep.

3. A converted attitude is the key to a transformed life.

4. We were meant to rule, govern, control, master, manage, and lead our environments.

5. You can fulfill your inherent leadership potential only when you understand who you are designed to be and discover the nature of a true leader.

6. Every human being has a natural inclination for leadership.

7. Most of our attitudes about leadership are a learned or conditioned response to erroneous ideas fostered by our families, cultures, and nations.

8. People's concepts of their origin often influence their ideas about their leadership potential.

9. The leadership implication of evolution is that those who are stronger—physically, intellectually, or creatively—are destined to lead and control others, while the rest are destined to be followers.

10. The leadership implication of creationism is that, regardless of our stations in life or current levels of skill, we all have leadership contributions to make in society according to our inherent domains.

11. Being made in the image and likeness of the Creator means having the Creator's nature, which is the spirit of leadership.

12. Five myths of leadership are: (1) Birth Trait Theory: "Leaders are born, not made"; (2) Leadership by Providence; (3) Leadership Is the Result of a Charismatic Personality; (4) Leadership Is the Product of a Forceful Personality; and (5) Leadership Is the Result of Special Training.

13. True leadership is an attitude that naturally inspires and motivates others.

14. Learning about leadership and knowing what it means to be a leader are two different things. Learning comes from education, while knowing comes from revelation. Learning is cognitive, while knowing is spiritual.

15. Most of us are not leaders because, in our hearts, we don't believe that is who we are.

16. The leadership spirit is our inherent leadership potential. The spirit of leadership is the consciousness of our being made in the image of our Creator, as well as the attitudes that accompany that awareness.

17. Every human being has the raw material for leadership, but most do not have the desire, courage, or will to use it.

18. True leadership is an attitude of the heart that is birthed by a renewed understanding of purpose.

19. You were *born* to lead, but you must *become* a leader.

CHAPTER TWO
WHAT IS A TRUE LEADER?

Leadership is the capacity to influence others through inspiration motivated by a passion, generated by a vision, produced by a conviction, ignited by a purpose.

P eter F. Drucker, one of our generation's foremost thinkers and authorities on the subject of leadership and management, stated, "There may be 'born leaders,' but there are surely far too few to depend on them. Leadership must be learned and can be learned....'leadership personality,' 'leadership style,' and 'leadership traits' do not exist."[3]

What makes a leader a leader? How do you identify leadership when it is present? In this chapter, we will explore various definitions of leadership and compare them with a definition of leadership that I have developed through years of observation and research. The examples of leaders that follow help demonstrate the fact that true leadership is an attitude rather than a title and that it inspires rather than manipulates or controls.

LEADERSHIP IS MORE THAN INFLUENCE

A popular definition of leadership is that "leadership is influence." In spite of the fact the leadership does involve the component of influence, I believe that this is an incomplete description because it does not distinguish what kind of influence or the source or cause of that influence.

Remember the story in chapter one of the teenage boy who had a gun and ordered everyone to "hit the ground"? What would you do in such a situation? You would probably do what he said because he would influence you to take a certain action through fear and intimidation, but I doubt you would consider his behavior to be leadership. The fact is that true leadership is not control or manipulation of others, but it is other people's willful submission of their authority to yours, motivated by inspiration.

TRUE LEADERSHIP IS MARKED BY OTHERS' WILLFUL SUBMISSION OF THEIR AUTHORITY TO YOURS.

There are many people, past and present, who have influenced others using threats and violence, but we don't call that true leadership. We call it manipulation, oppression, or dictatorship. Nero, Hitler, and Idi Amin were all influential. They exerted their wills over people, but they were not leaders in the true sense.

A WORKING DEFINITION OF LEADERSHIP

True leadership fundamentally requires the responsibility of taking followers into the exciting unknown and creating a new reality for them. For over thirty years, I have dedicated myself to the study of the subject of leadership. After thousands of hours of study, research, and reading hundreds of books on the subject, I determined to craft my own comprehensive definition of leadership as I have come to understand it. This definition incorporates the principal ingredients and components that I believe give birth to and sustain true leadership and can be applied by anyone who desires to discover and release the hidden leader within. The following is my definition of leadership, which will serve as the working definition of leadership throughout this book:

Leadership is the capacity to influence others through inspiration motivated by a passion, generated by a vision, produced by a conviction, ignited by a purpose.

THE PRIORITY OF INSPIRATION

A careful study of this definition will reveal that leadership is not a pursuit but a result. Under this definition, the word *leader* is not a label that you give yourself. *Leader* is what the people whom you inspire call you because they are stirred to participate in the positive vision that you are presenting them—whether it is the vision for a country, a company, or a cause.

Leadership is a privilege given by the followers. The great Jewish rabbi, Jesus of Nazareth—the ultimate model of effective leadership—inspired his chosen followers so much that they left their businesses and, for a time, their families, in order to follow him. He never threatened them or forced them to come, but he inspired them and then invited them to join him.

A further study of this definition will also reveal the priority of *inspiration* in the development of a leader and his leadership. In fact, **true leadership is one hundred**

percent influence through inspiration. The principal pursuit, therefore, for those who desire and aspire to become effective leaders must be the answer to this question: "How do I inspire and what is the source of inspiration?"

LEADERSHIP IS NOT A PURSUIT BUT A RESULT.

The best way to approach and appreciate the practical application of our definition is to start the process at the end of the definition. You will note that the process begins with an individual's discovery of a personal *purpose* that, when captured, ignites a conviction. This conviction generates a vision in the person's heart that stirs a passion. The force of this person's passionate pursuit of the vision inspires others, who are stirred to join in and cooperate with the vision. This ultimate effect is called "influence" and results in the followers acknowledging the individual as their "leader."

If inspiration is the key to legitimate influence and thus the source of true leadership, then, again, inspiration should be the pursuit of all true leaders. How do leaders inspire others? What is the source of inspiration? These are the most important questions of leadership, and when you have found the answer to them, then you will have begun to discover your own leadership potential.

THE POWER OF PASSION

Simply put, the source of inspiration is *passion*. This component of leadership is the heart of influence and is the generator of the energy and resilience of the leader.

Passion is the discovery of a deep desire born out of a conviction that renders one possessed by commitment to a purpose. This passionate commitment allows one to defy opposition, adversity, failure, disappointment, and discouragement.

Passion is a controlling desire that exceeds the boundaries of casual interest or concern and transports the individual into the realm of obligation. In essence, **true leadership passion is the discovery of a belief, reason, idea, conviction, or cause not just to live for, but also to die for, which focuses on benefiting mankind as a whole.** It is this sense of personal resolve, obligation, and willingness to sacrifice personal advantage, comfort, and advancement for the sake of a noble cause that impacts others and resonates within them a desire to help achieve the stated desire, goal, or vision. True leaders, therefore, are those who effectively express their inner passions, which find a common response in the hearts of others. It is passion that attracts people to the leader, who motivates them to take action.

This vital aspect of effective leadership development was expressed in the lives of all great leaders throughout history and identifies what separates them from their followers. Again, consider the greatest leader of all time, the young Jewish rabbi Jesus Christ, who personifies our definition of true leadership. His leadership effectiveness is undisputed even by his critics and skeptics, and no study of historical leaders can be fairly conducted without reference to his impeccable achievement and his model as a leader of the highest order. No man has ever affected the destiny and development of humanity as this one.

WHAT IS A TRUE LEADER?

THE ULTIMATE LEADERSHIP MODEL

Born in an obscure, forgotten town in the hills of ancient Judea; raised in a village that, according to archeological research, had only one street and eleven houses; and leaving no record of having had any formal education, this young man introduced his vision of a new world order to simple village people who themselves were considered least on the social strata. Yet his clear sense of purpose, his commitment to the cause, and his unrelenting passion and compassion inspired twelve common local businessmen—among them, four fishermen and a tax collector—to abandon their personal dreams, private priorities, and occupations to follow him even to the death.

THE SOURCE OF TRUE PASSION IS THE DISCOVERY OF A CLEAR SENSE OF PURPOSE.

He was so passionate about what he came to do that he motivated his disciples to leave behind their old priorities and ways of living in order to discover a new kind of life with him. They had never before met anyone who was ready to die for what he was living for. Moreover, his impact and imprint on the history of the world and on the personal lives of millions over two millennia testify of leadership at its highest and in its essence.

As I mentioned earlier, the source of true passion is the discovery of a clear sense of purpose and significance for one's life. When a person discovers a sense of purpose, it produces a passion for pursuing it, and that passion is what inspires other people to want to join in the pursuit. Then, as people are inspired, their thinking and their lives are naturally influenced. True inspiration is not manipulation or brainwashing. Instead, it is an invitation to pursue something higher and better than one has had before and, in the process, gain a sense of meaning and significance for one's life.

To clarify the process of leadership according to our working definition, let us review the progression of leadership development:

1. Purpose
2. Conviction
3. Vision
4. Passion
5. Inspiration
6. Influence
7. Leadership

True leadership is impossible unless all these ingredients are present and integrated as a whole, producing a force for change in our communities, societies, and the world.

Examples of Effective Leaders

Leaders are often ordinary people who accept or are placed in extraordinary circumstances that bring forth their latent potential, producing a character that inspires confidence and trust within others. Many of the great leaders in history were "victims" of circumstances. They did not intend to be leaders, but the demands of life ignited a sleeping spirit within them. **The greatest leadership seems to surface during times of personal, social, economic, political, and spiritual conflict.**

WHAT IS A TRUE LEADER?

Let's look again at the definition of leadership that I am proposing:

Leadership is the capacity to influence others through inspiration motivated by a passion, generated by a vision, produced by a conviction, ignited by a purpose.

When you apply this definition of leadership to every one of the following people, you begin to see a common thread that explains their leadership influence. I have interspersed examples of great leaders from ancient and contemporary times. Each of these leaders first discovered a purpose for their lives that became a passion. Their passion inspired and influenced others who personally embraced the leaders' purposes and allowed these leaders to guide them in the specific direction of their visions, which brought about changes in the world.

LEADERS ARE OFTEN ORDINARY PEOPLE WHO ARE PLACED IN EXTRAORDINARY CIRCUMSTANCES.

MOSES

Moses, the historic Hebrew deliverer, was given a clear sense of purpose. In his writings, he described his encounter with God in the wilderness where he was told what he had been born to accomplish: freeing his fellow Hebrews, who were slaves in Egypt, and leading them to a promised land. After some initial apprehension concerning the details of his assignment, Moses became passionate about his purpose. He described it to his brother, Aaron, who went with him to the Israelites and told them about this vision of a promised land. Moses believed in his purpose so deeply that they, also, began to believe that their freedom was possible. He inspired them to have the courage to abandon their painful, but accustomed, role of being a slave labor force in Egypt. The result was that they were willing to follow him out into the desert where there was no civilization and no source of food or water. They had caught the vision for this Land that Moses told them about, a "land flowing with milk and honey," and were influenced to follow him into the unknown wilderness with confidence.

MARTIN LUTHER KING JR.

The unforgettable speech, "I Have a Dream," encapsulates the purpose, passion, and inspiration of Dr. Martin Luther King Jr. A leader and symbol of American blacks' struggle for civil rights, Dr. King helped to change both laws and hearts in America, leading to greater equality and freedom in the country. Here are some of his inspirational words from that speech:

> I have a dream that one day this nation will rise up and live out the true meaning of its creed: "We hold these truths to be self-evident; that all men are created equal."

> ...I have a dream that my four little children will one day live in a nation where they will not be judged by the color of their skin but by the content of their character.[4]

Dr. King's purpose was the pursuit of equality, and his conviction and passion were a vision of his country, the United States, in which freedom was every person's right and privilege. His passion became an obligation that set him on a course of self-sacrifice. Hundreds of thousands of people caught his vision, which became not only his destiny, but also that of a whole nation, as he influenced a change in the fundamental laws of the land. Dr. King had a vision that he was willing to live—and die—for.

SIR WINSTON CHURCHILL

During World War II, before the United States entered the war, Great Britain was an underdog, fighting single-handedly to save not only England, but also most of Europe, from being overrun and ruled by Nazi Germany. Their leader was Winston Churchill, who was considered washed up in politics before becoming prime minister at the age of sixty-six. Later, he wrote, "I felt as if I was walking with destiny, and that all my past life had been but a preparation for this hour and for this trial."[5]

"NEVER GIVEN IN, NEVER GIVE IN—*NEVER, NEVER, NEVER, NEVER.*"

Winston Churchill's speeches during this time of national crisis reveal his sense of purpose. He inspired the English people to believe that parliamentary democracy and freedom were valuable enough to fight and even die for. His purpose produced a tireless passion to prevail, and his confident, cheerful manner and powerful speeches are credited with keeping the morale of the English people strong when they faced seemingly impossible odds. One of his most famous sayings was, "Never give in, never give in, *never, never, never, never*—in nothing, great or small, large or petty—never give in except to convictions of honour and good sense."[6] His speech, "Their Finest Hour," is clear evidence of his ability to inspire those who were looking to him for leadership:

...the Battle of France is over. I expect that the Battle of Britain is about to begin. Upon this battle depends the survival of Christian civilization. Upon it depends our own British life and the long continuity of our institutions and our Empire. The whole fury and might of the enemy must very soon be turned on us. Hitler knows that he will have to break us in this Island or lose the war. If we can stand up to him, all Europe may be free and the life of the world may move forward into broad, sunlit uplands. But if we fail, then the whole world, including the United States, including all that we have known and cared for, will sink into the abyss of a new Dark Age....

Let us therefore brace ourselves to our duties, and so bear ourselves that, if the British Empire and its Commonwealth last for a thousand years, men will still say, "*This* was their finest hour."[7]

Churchill's vision for Great Britain and the world influenced both individuals and nations to extend themselves beyond what they thought they were capable of in order to achieve victory.

NEHEMIAH

Nehemiah was a Jewish exile who was serving as cupbearer to the Persian king Artaxerxes. He had a visit from some men from Judah who told him that the wall of Jerusalem was broken down and that its gates had been burned. Grieved at this state of affairs and what it symbolized about the plight of his people, Nehemiah prayed night and day. He believed that God had put it into his heart to do something about the situation. Rebuilding the wall became his purpose, which created an all-consuming passion to restore what he could of the city. His deep passion influenced Artaxerxes—who had no real reason to want to rebuild the city of people his nation had conquered—to help Nehemiah fulfill his desire. He provided his cupbearer with safe passage to Jerusalem and even supplied building materials.

Nehemiah traveled to Jerusalem and told the Jews living in the region about his vision to rebuild the wall and how King Artaxerxes himself was helping him. His personal commitment to the restoration of Jerusalem inspired the people, and they readily joined him in the work.

Nehemiah soon faced bitter opposition from some of the local residents and officials. When Nehemiah's enemies tried to lure him from the project, he remained focused on his purpose, essentially saying, "I am doing a great work. Why should the work cease while I leave it and come down to you?" When he and his fellow-workers were threatened with fear, intimidation, and physical attack, his steadfastness and belief in their God-given purpose inspired them to hold firmly to the vision and refuse to give way until the task was completed. His leadership was the result of the discovery of a purpose that produced a vision and deep passion, which influenced an entire population to rally to a cause that benefited the whole nation and changed the course of history.

QUEEN ESTHER

Esther was a beautiful young Hebrew woman, also living in exile, but at a slightly earlier time period. Through an extraordinary set of circumstances, she became the queen of the Persian king Ahasuerus, also known as Xerxes. When she learned of a plot to annihilate the Jews, she discovered that she had been born for a critical purpose: preserving her people. Her uncle told her, in effect, "Perhaps you have become queen for such a time as this."

When Esther accepted her purpose, it became her passion, and she was willing to risk her own life for its fulfillment, saying, "If I perish, I perish." Her courage and grace under tremendous pressure influenced the king to agree to a plan to protect the Jews, who were inspired to rally to defend themselves.

"PERHAPS YOU ARE A LEADER FOR SUCH A TIME AS THIS."

Esther was an ordinary woman who was placed in extraordinary circumstances and had a part in influencing and preserving her whole generation. Her sense of purpose and destiny was clear and produced in her a passion for which she was willing to die. This passion impacted and influenced the king and saved a whole nation under her leadership.

NELSON MANDELA

Nelson Mandela's life purpose was the elimination of the policy of apartheid and the establishment of racial equality in South Africa. He desired the formation of a free and democratic society for all people, black and white. His passion for this purpose led him to fight for these causes, for which he was sentenced to life in prison. At his trial, he explained his vision for his country:

I have fought against white domination and I have fought against black domination. I have cherished the ideal of a democratic and free society in which all persons live together in harmony and with equal opportunities. It is an ideal which I hope to live for and to achieve. But if needs be, it is an ideal for which I am prepared to die."[8]

Following national and international pressure, Mandela was released from prison after twenty-eight years. He then worked with South Africa's white leader, F. W. de Klerk, to eliminate apartheid, and they both were awarded the Nobel Peace Prize in 1993. In a historic event, Mandela was elected president of his country under open democratic elections and served in that position from 1994–1999. Mandela's passion transformed an entire country's outlook, government, structure, and policies.

It was Mandela's sense of purpose as a young lawyer that produced a vision of a new South Africa without discrimination and racism. This purpose and vision ignited a deep passion that exploded into a sacrificial flame of imprisonment and a willingness to die for his convictions. His vision inspired not only millions in his country, but also countless millions around the world. It is important to recognize that true leaders do not seek or pursue followers but instead attract them by their dedication to a personal purpose.

KING DAVID

David is one of the most fascinating and remarkable leaders in the history of the world. His lifelong purpose was a desire to serve his God, restore the honor of his nation, and strengthen his people politically and militarily.

When King Saul of Israel turned his back on God, the prophet Samuel was sent to anoint David—the youngest-born of a humble Israelite family—as king. At this time, David was just a young shepherd boy. Only Samuel, David, and David's family knew about this anointing, and it would be many years before David would be recognized as king. However, the biblical account says that David was "a man after God's own heart." David's purpose and passion were recognized as valuable qualities in the man who would lead the Israelite nation.

TRUE LEADERS DO NOT SEEK OR PURSUE FOLLOWERS BUT INSTEAD ATTRACT THEM.

David was passionate about his purpose, and he leapt to prominence soon after his anointing. He was the only one who believed that the Israelites could defeat their enemies, the Philistines, including the colossal Philistine warrior Goliath—whose coat of mail alone weighed two hundred pounds.

David asked, in essence, "Who is this who defies the armies of the living God?" Using merely a slingshot and five smooth rocks, he released a well-aimed missile that hit the giant in the forehead, instantly killing him. The Israelites then routed the Philistine army. David inspired not only the army, but also the whole nation, to believe that they were not victims but were able to overcome their enemies. David subsequently became a military hero and was a favorite in the court of King Saul, whose son, Jonathan, became his best friend.

Yet David's success on the battlefield set up a long and intense decade of conflict and exile for him. He and his loyal followers were continually running for their lives as Saul, in his jealousy, sought to kill David. All during this time, David continually respected Saul as king and preserved his life even when he twice had an opportunity to kill him.

Eventually, Saul and Jonathan were killed in a battle against the Philistines, and David finally began to reign as king. Under David's rule, the nation grew and prospered. The foundation was set for its becoming one of the most respected, feared, and powerful nations in the world. Before his death, David helped prepare materials for the magnificent temple in Jerusalem, which his son, Solomon, constructed.

David inspired his people through his devotion, his faith, his loyalty, and his bravery. In response, his people loved, respected, and served him. Even today, thousands of years later, millions continue to be inspired by the record of the stories and events of his life, which depict his deep sense of purpose and passion.

ABRAHAM LINCOLN

Abraham Lincoln believed that it was essential for the future of the United States to keep the country united at a time when the Southern states wanted to secede over the issues of slavery and states' rights. His purpose was to preserve the Union, and his passion to do so led him to hold on to his vision of a unified country, even when it led to civil war. He, too, had a purpose for which he was willing to die. Lincoln wrote,

I have often inquired of myself what great principle
or idea it was that kept this Confederacy [Union]
so long together....It was that which gave promise
that in due time the weight would be lifted from the
shoulders of all men. This is a sentiment embodied
in the Declaration of Independence....

I have said nothing but what I am willing to live
by and, if it be the pleasure of Almighty God, die
by.[9]

Lincoln also helped to influence the nation to throw
off the yoke of slavery. Just before Lincoln's Emancipation
Proclamation went into effect, he announced his purpose and passion for his action in his annual message to
Congress:

The fiery trial through which we pass, will light us
down, in honor or dishonor, to the latest generation....We—even *we here*—hold the power, and bear
the responsibility. In *giving* freedom to the *slave*, we
assure freedom to the *free*—honorable alike in what
we give, and what we preserve. We shall nobly save,
or meanly lose, the last best hope of earth. Other
means may succeed; this could not fail. The way
is plain, peaceful, generous, just—a way which, if
followed, the world will forever applaud, and God
must forever bless.[10]

Finally, Lincoln inspired people to bring an end to the
war and to restore the unity of the country, even though
his purpose did, indeed, eventually cost him his life.

Fondly do we hope—fervently do we pray—that this
mighty scourge of war may speedily pass away....

With malice toward none; with charity for all; with firmness in the right, as God gives us to see the right, let us strive on to finish the work we are in; to bind up the nation's wounds...to do all which may achieve and cherish a just and lasting peace, among ourselves, and with all nations.[11]

CORRIE TEN BOOM

Corrie ten Boom was fifty years old when the Nazis invaded her native Holland. Up to that time, she had lived an obscure life with her sister as they helped their father run his watch shop and quietly but devotedly practiced their Christian faith. After Holland fell, she and her family were confronted with the reality of the Nazis' persecution and murder of the Jews. Through this crisis, they discovered their purpose: preserving the lives of Jews and others persecuted by the Nazis by hiding them in a secret room in their home. Their passion was so strong that they risked their own lives for its fulfillment.

PASSION CAN BE SO STRONG THAT IT LEADS MEN AND WOMEN TO RISK THEIR LIVES FOR ITS FULFILLMENT.

Corrie and several of her family members were eventually turned in. The Gestapo never found the Jews and members of the Dutch underground who were hiding in their house at the time of their arrest, and the refugees were taken to new "safe houses." However, Corrie's father died in prison and her sister died in a concentration camp. After suffering in prison, a work camp, and a concentration camp, Corrie was about to be executed when she was released on a clerical error.

After her release, Corrie found a new purpose. Traveling around the world, she told her story and urged people to find healing and freedom through forgiveness. This purpose was severely tested when she encountered one of the former guards who had beaten her beloved sister. He didn't recognize her, but he had heard her message and been moved to change his life through the hope of forgiveness. He came and extended his hand to her. Corrie underwent intense inner struggle, but her passion was even stronger than her pain, and she offered her own hand in forgiveness.

Corrie ten Boom's faith, courage, and personal strength have inspired millions who have read her book or seen the movie based on her life, both called *The Hiding Place*.

JOHN F. KENNEDY

When John F. Kennedy was president of the United States, he demonstrated clear purpose in two major areas: He felt that he had to do something to help the poor and disadvantaged at home and abroad, and he felt that he had to develop an effective space program, placing America in the forefront of nations in regard to science and technology. Those two things, in my view, define his passion. In both pursuits, he felt his purpose was to create a sense of dignity for the American psyche.

As a result, JFK inspired the nation to take care of those who were less fortunate, exemplified by his statement, "Ask not what your country can do for you, but what you can do for your country." In other words, he was asking his countrymen to serve others rather than just themselves. To give

Americans a concrete way to do this, he initiated the Peace Corps program, which sends volunteers to help nationals in underdeveloped nations.

Kennedy also inspired the United States to invest billions of dollars in a space program. I believe that he first created in his countrymen American pride, and then he strengthened that self-image by enabling the American people to achieve what no nation had ever achieved— sending a manned spaceship to the moon and back.

RONALD REAGAN

Ronald Reagan had a clear sense of his life's purpose: the elimination of Communism. He desired to lift totalitarian oppression from millions of people who were suffering under its ideology and policies. His purpose became his passion, and it influenced his thinking, his pursuits, and his foreign policies as president of the United States. Unlike previous American leaders, he believed that Communism not only could be contained, but that it could also be defeated.

OUR PURPOSE MUST BECOME OUR PASSION, INFLUENCING OUR THINKING AND PURSUITS.

It is time that we committed ourselves as a nation— in both the public and private sectors—to assisting democratic development....

What I am describing now is a plan and a hope for the long term—the march of freedom and democracy which will leave Marxism-Leninism on the ash heap of history as it has left other tyrannies which stifle the freedom and muzzle the self-expression of the people....

Let us now begin a major effort to secure the best—a crusade for freedom that will engage the faith and fortitude of the next generation. For the sake of peace and justice, let us move toward a world in which all people are at last free to determine their own destiny.[12]

Like Churchill, Reagan became the leader of his country late in life, but everything he experienced and accomplished up to that point seemed to prepare him for his final and essential role. Delivering one of his most memorable quotes, Reagan stood before the Berlin Wall, a highly visible symbol of communist oppression, and directed this statement to Mikhail Gorbachev, then president of the Soviet Union, which controlled East Germany: "Mr. Gorbachev, tear down this wall!"

Reagan believed in his purpose so much that he inspired not only his nation, but also the world, and he lived to see the collapse of Communism.

PAUL

Paul, the early Christian leader and writer, was dedicated to the purpose of taking the message of Christianity to the Gentile peoples. At first passionately opposed to the Way, as Christianity was then called, Paul received his purpose on a roadway to Damascus when he had an encounter with the living Christ.

Paul's life was turned 180 degrees. He discovered that he was born to become an emissary to people who were not of his own race and culture. His passion for this purpose can be found in his letter to the early Christians of Rome, in which he wrote that he was "obligated both to Greeks and non-Greeks," and that he was "eager to preach" to them. He also stated, "I am not ashamed of the gospel."

CONVICTION ABOUT YOUR LIFE PURPOSE LEADS YOU TO KEEP GOING IN THE MIDST OF OBSTACLES.

First, he said that he was "obligated," or compelled, by an inner purpose to go to the Gentile peoples. Second, he was "eager." His purpose generated an excitement and anticipation for carrying out his work. Third, he was "not ashamed" of his task. No matter how much ridicule, persecution, or danger he faced, he always persevered in his calling.

How many people have such conviction about their life's purpose that they keep going in the midst of odds and obstacles such as those Paul faced? He couldn't have done it without both inner purpose and passion. In his second letter to the church in the city of Corinth in ancient Greece, he wrote of his continual hard work and how he was whipped, beaten with rods, stoned, hunted by the authorities, imprisoned, and constantly in danger of death. He was shipwrecked three times; one of those times, he was adrift at sea for twenty-four hours before coming to safety. He described being "constantly on the move," facing danger from rivers, bandits, his own countrymen, and Gentiles. He also said,

> I have labored and toiled and have often gone without sleep; I have known hunger and thirst and have often gone without food; I have been cold and naked.

Besides everything else, I face daily the pressure of my concern for all the churches. Who is weak, and I do not feel weak?...If I must boast, I will boast of the things that show my weakness.

Paul's dedication to his purpose and genuine love for the people he served inspired not only his generation, but also succeeding generations who, for two thousand years, have read his words and been influenced by his vision and example. This is the essence of true leadership—purpose, conviction, passion, inspiration, and commitment unto death.

MOTHER TERESA

Agnes Gonxha Bojaxhiu, whom the world has come to know as Mother Teresa, was born in Skopje, Macedonia. From the time she was a girl, she felt her life's purpose was to serve God full-time. When she was eighteen, she became a nun and went to India with the Sisters of Loreto and taught in a Catholic high school for many years. During this time, she witnessed the life of poverty and sickness that many people in India were leading. Her life's purpose and passion crystallized as she felt called by God to help "the poorest of the poor" and devoted herself to bring hope, dignity, healing, and education to the needy in Calcutta—those whom other people dismissed as being either beyond help or not worthy of it.

Mother Teresa started her own order called "The Missionaries of Charity" and became nationally and internationally recognized for her selfless humanitarian work. Her passion to help others led her to identify totally with them: She became a citizen of India and always kept her vow of poverty, even when she became famous.

Her work expanded beyond India to other nations of the world, influencing hundreds of thousands of people to join in her vision. She believed in the difference that one person could make in the world, saying, "If you can't feed a hundred people, then just feed one," and "Love is a fruit in season at all times, and within reach of every hand."[13] Mother Teresa was awarded the Nobel Peace Prize in 1979 and continued her work until her death in the 1990s.

"DO NOT WAIT FOR LEADERS; DO IT ALONE, PERSON TO PERSON."

Mother Teresa encouraged others, "Do not wait for leaders; do it alone, person to person."[14] This statement seems to sum up her purpose, passion, and inspiration: In not waiting for leaders to initiate programs or other people to act when there was a real need, but instead doing what she personally could do to help, Mother Teresa became a leader herself. She influenced numerous others to awaken their own leadership gifts and, in so doing, multiplied her effectiveness thousands of times over. Again, we note that true leaders do not seek followers, but their passionate pursuit of their purposes and convictions inspire others to follow them in their declared vision.

DISCOVERING YOUR PERSONAL LEADERSHIP POTENTIAL

Mother Teresa's story reemphasizes this important truth in regard to leadership: We must remember that, while leaders have followers, having followers is not a prerequisite for being a leader. **The demands of leadership may require that you stand alone in the face of conflict, public opinion,**

or crisis. Then, that very willingness to stand for what you believe in, no matter what, is what often inspires people to follow.

Most leaders go against the grain, at one point or another, and have to stand alone in their convictions. For example, Nelson Mandela was willing to die or be imprisoned alone to fulfill his passion to end apartheid. His determination inspired many people to keep believing during all the years that he was incarcerated. When he was finally released from prison, he went on to influence the world because of his courage. If you want to be a leader, then, as Mother Teresa said, "Do not wait for [other] leaders; do it alone, person to person." When you have a purpose and a passion, you must act on it, even if you're the only one who believes in it at the time.

MOST LEADERS HAVE TO GO AGAINST THE GRAIN AT ONE POINT OR ANOTHER.

The previous examples demonstrate that the purest form of leadership is influence through inspiration. **I think of inspiration as the divine deposit of destiny in the heart of a person. It is the opposite of intimidation, and it contains no manipulation.**

Let's summarize this section with another definition of leadership that describes the lives we've just looked at: "Leadership is the capacity to influence, inspire, rally, direct, encourage, motivate, induce, move, mobilize, and activate others to pursue a common goal or purpose while maintaining commitment, momentum, confidence, and courage."

How do you discover your own purpose and passion—
your personal "divine deposit of destiny"? A very important way is to ask yourself, "What is my gifting?" What you
are gifted in often reveals the type of leadership you are
meant to exercise and what domain you are to operate in.[15]
**True leaders discover keys to the nature of leadership
from the examples of others, but they never try to _become_
these other leaders. They must use their own gifts and
abilities to do what they are individually called to do.**

THE VITAL NEED FOR YOUR LEADERSHIP

If you do not discover your personal leadership potential, this means that you will not be able to fulfill your
life's assignment. The result is that you will deprive your
generation and succeeding generations of your unique and
vital contribution to the world. I believe that the Creator
has given each one of us life in order to accomplish something in our generation. The great king Solomon wrote
that there is "a time to be born and a time to die." This
means that the timing of your birth was essential to some
need in the world that you're supposed to meet.

Suppose Moses had refused to go to Egypt and tell
Pharaoh to set the Hebrews free. Consider what the world
would be like if Winston Churchill had said, "The survival
of Great Britain and the rest of the free world is someone
else's problem. I'm going to let the Nazis do whatever they
want." Suppose Corrie ten Boom had decided that hiding
Jews was too risky a proposition. What if Martin Luther
King Jr. had not thought civil rights were worth dying for?
What would have happened if Mother Teresa had ignored
the poor and sick on the streets of Calcutta?

We may never know in our lifetimes the full impact of our influence and actions, great or small. In light of this truth, developing one's leadership potential should not be an option for anyone. We have a responsibility to find, perform, and complete our purposes. As we come to understand the nature and attitudes of true leaders, we can remove whatever is hindering us from having the spirit of leadership so that we can make a positive and lasting contribution to our generation.

CHAPTER PRINCIPLES

1. True leadership is an attitude rather than a title. It inspires rather than manipulates or controls.

2. Influence alone is not leadership. Leadership is the capacity to influence others through inspiration motivated by a passion, generated by a vision, produced by a conviction, ignited by a purpose.

3. Leadership is not a pursuit but a result.

4. *Leader* is not a label that you give yourself. Leadership is a privilege given by the followers.

5. Leaders inspire by expressing their inner passion, which then resonates with others and causes them to join in pursuing the leaders' visions.

6. The source of inspiration is passion.

7. True leadership passion is the discovery of a belief, reason, idea, conviction, or cause not just to live for, but also to die for, which focuses on benefiting mankind as a whole.

8. Passion comes from purpose.

9. True inspiration is not manipulation or brainwashing but an invitation to pursue something higher and better than one has had before, and in the process gain a sense of meaning and significance for one's life.

10. Leaders are often ordinary people who accept or are placed under extraordinary circumstances that bring forth their latent potential, producing a character that inspires confidence and trust within others.

11. The greatest leadership seems to surface during times of personal, social, economic, political, and spiritual conflict.

12. Having followers is not a prerequisite for being a leader. The demands of leadership may require that you stand alone in the face of conflict, public opinion, or crisis.

13. Inspiration is the "divine deposit of destiny" in the heart of a person.

14. What you are gifted in often reveals what type of leadership you are meant to exercise and what domain you are to operate in.

15. True leaders discover keys to the nature of leadership from the examples of others, but they never try to *become* these other leaders. They use their own gifts and abilities to do what they are individually called to do.

16. Failing to discover or pursue your personal leadership potential will deprive your generation and succeeding generations of your unique and vital contribution to the world.

CHAPTER THREE
THE LEADERSHIP SPIRIT

*To exercise leadership, you must believe
that you are inherently a leader.*

L eadership really comes down to two things: who you are and how you think. It is about discovering your identity as a born leader and then understanding the way true leaders think so that you can fulfill your inherent calling. If you don't first establish your leadership nature, it will be very difficult to have the mind-set of leadership.

True leadership is first concerned with who you are, as opposed to what you do. Leadership action flows naturally from a personal leadership revelation. To exercise leadership, you must believe that you are inherently a leader. Again, to pursue purpose as leaders do, you must think like a leader. To think like a leader, you must receive the thoughts of leadership. To receive the thoughts of leadership, you must have a personal encounter with your true self—a discovery of your nature, ability, and essence as a human being. Just as a product cannot know its true purpose or worth except in its relationship with its manufacturer, so it is with you and me.

Earlier, I made a distinction between the leadership spirit and the spirit of leadership. **The *leadership spirit* is**

the inherent leadership capacity and potential that is the essential nature of human beings. The *spirit of leadership*, which is what most of this book focuses on, is the mind-set or attitudes that accompany a true leadership spirit and allow the dormant leadership potential to be fully manifested and maximized. Clearly understanding this difference is critical for discovering and living out your leadership capacity. In this chapter, we'll take a closer look at the leadership spirit. In the next chapter, we will explore the spirit of leadership.

LEADERSHIP COMES DOWN TO TWO THINGS: WHO YOU ARE AND HOW YOU THINK.

WHAT IS THE LEADERSHIP SPIRIT?

In my leadership lectures and seminars, which I share with governmental, educational, business, nonprofit, and religious organizations around the world, I usually begin with a statement that encapsulates my philosophy of leadership: "**Trapped within every follower is a hidden leader.**" I am always amused to watch the reaction on the faces of the audiences as they attempt to grapple with the implications of this statement. I can usually predict their first thought, which is often the question, "If every follower is a potential leader, then who is going to follow?" This reaction is natural and legitimate in light of our traditional concepts and philosophy of leadership, as they have been promoted over the centuries.

However, the above statement contains the essence of what the original philosophy of leadership was intended to be. It is upon this premise that I propose the belief that leadership is inherent in the human spirit of every person, but only a minute fraction of the human population ever knows, discovers, believes, or attempts to develop or release this hidden leadership potential.

This leadership capacity is buried under social, cultural, and ideological perceptions that restrict, discourage, and hinder its manifestation. The majority of this planet's population surrenders to the social concept of leadership and cowers in the shadows of the myths of leadership philosophy. The result is that their tremendous gifts and talents are stifled, and the world is never able to benefit from them. What a tragedy.

My awareness of this suppression of our leadership gifting gave birth to the deep purpose in my heart, which has become the passion of my life: to help as many people as possible, of every nation, race, creed, or social status, to discover their true leadership potential.

LEADERSHIP: THE INHERENT CAPACITY OF THE HUMAN SPIRIT

If trapped in every follower is a hidden leader, then from where did this inherent leadership potential come? And if it exists, why do so many never seem to exhibit it or show some evidence of its presence? These questions point to the heart of the theme of this book, which is *the leadership spirit.*

A complete definition of the leadership spirit would be—

The inherent capacity of the human spirit to lead, manage, and dominate, which was placed there at the point of creation and made necessary by the purpose and assignment for which man (humanity) was created.

To understand this concept and its underlying principle, it is necessary to understand the principles inherent in the nature of creation. Again, leadership is not something that human beings should *strive* for; it is something that we already have been given because of our purpose and design. The leadership spirit is the essence of the human spirit. Man doesn't *have* a spirit; man *is* a spirit, and that spirit is an expression of God's Spirit. The essential nature of his Spirit is in our spirits because of the Source from which we come. Leadership is really a discovery of who we truly are and the application of that discovery to our lives. Simply put, true leadership is self-discovery and self-manifestation.

WHEN WE BECOME OUR TRUE SELVES, WE WILL NATURALLY BE LEADERS.

Recognizing the leadership spirit is key to understanding ourselves. We don't actually "become" leaders, as if leadership were an option among other choices. Rather, **when we become our true selves, we will naturally *be* leaders.** We will desire to maximize all our gifts and talents in the fulfillment of our purposes in life. To understand this critical point, however, we must study the source of the leadership spirit.

THE SOURCE OF THE LEADERSHIP SPIRIT

To help you understand the principle of the creation of the leadership spirit, let me begin with an illustration.

In 1976, I was a student at a renowned university, and one of my major areas of study was fine art. In this course of study, we had to produce paintings, stone sculptures, drawings, and artwork in a variety of media. I loved the stone and wood sculpture work and learned many lessons from the experience. However, one of the most significant lessons I learned concerned the principles of source and resource and their relation to purpose and potential. These lessons have cultivated and formed the foundation of my under-standing of and my philosophy of life.

On two occasions, I set about working on a wood and stone sculpture project and chose my raw material from dis-carded pieces of tree and stone. After laboring many hours following the design I had developed, the day came when I was finally finished and proud of the results. When I sub-mitted my project to the professor, I obtained an A and was successful in fulfilling my requirements for graduation. I was so proud of my sculptures that I took them home with me and placed them in a very prominent place in my apart-ment.

A year later, however, something happened that changed the life of my sculptures forever. I decided to clean the wooden sculpture and wax the stonework. As I picked up the wooden piece to shine the results of my hard work, part of the wood stayed on the table and the other part came off in my hands. My heart sank as the bottom of the figure then gave way and fell apart right before my eyes.

Deeply shocked at this turn of events, I moved to the stone sculpture and wondered if the same thing would happen. As I rubbed it lightly with the cloth, the stone began to come apart like dust. With great disappointment and despair, I had to accept the reality that all my work had been in vain and that the rest of my artwork was destined for disintegration. Today, both pieces are only memories, but I cherish more the lesson this experience taught me.

Here is the great wisdom I gained from the wood and stone sculptures:

1. The nature of the composition of the source material determines the nature of the composition of the product made or produced from it.

2. Whatever is in the source is in the product.

3. The strength and durability of the source determines the durability of the product made from it.

4. The ability of the product is only as good as the ability of its source.

5. If the source is porous and weak, then the product will be porous and weak.

6. The key principle is that a thing consists of the same components and consistency as that from which it came. In other words,

7. Source determines resource.

PRINCIPLES OF CREATION

These insights helped me to understand the nature of life itself and, as a result, changed my life. A careful review of the creation account in the first book of Moses in the Hebrew Scriptures reveals that everything in creation was created from a specific raw material or source. In the first chapter of the account, we observe the process and principles of creation as the Creator produces the many products of nature, such as stars, vegetation, animals, sea creatures, and birds. The important precepts hidden in these creative acts may be summarized in the following principles:

1. The Creator first established the purpose of whatever he desired to make.

2. The Creator identified the material from which each product in creation was to be made.

3. The Creator directed his creative speech to the material from which he desired the product to be made.

4. The product possessed the same components as the source from which it was derived, and therefore possessed the same potential.

SOURCE DETERMINES RESOURCE.

From the following creation Scriptures, we quickly notice that everything that lives on the Earth was somehow sourced by the Earth and thus consists of the Earth's elements:

> Then God said, "Let the land produce vegetation: seed-bearing plants and trees on the land that bear fruit with seed in it, according to their various kinds." And it was so. The land produced vegetation: plants bearing seed according to their kinds and trees bearing fruit with seed in it according to their kinds. And God saw that it was good.

> And God said, "Let the water teem with living creatures, and let birds fly above the earth across the expanse of the sky." So God created the great creatures of the sea and every living and moving thing with which the water teems, according to their kinds, and every winged bird according to its kind. And God saw that it was good.

And God said, "Let the land produce living creatures according to their kinds: livestock, creatures that move along the ground, and wild animals, each according to its kind." And it was so. God made the wild animals according to their kinds, the livestock according to their kinds, and all the creatures that move along the ground according to their kinds. And God saw that it was good.

Vegetation, birds, and animals, in essence, came from the soil. Fish and other sea creatures were created from the waters, and the stars were produced out of the firmament. All the wonderful products of creation that we have on Earth consist of whatever their source is, and when they die, they, in effect, return to the components of that source. In the case of plants and animals, they return to the dust from which they came.

Why is this principle so important to understanding the leadership spirit? The answer in found in the Creator's process of creating mankind. When the above aspects of nature were made, the Creator directed his creative speech to the soil, water, or firmament. But when it came to creating the human species, his focus changed.

Then God said, "Let us make man in our image, in our likeness, and let them rule ["have dominion"] over the fish of the sea and the birds of the air, over the livestock, over all the earth, and over all the creatures that move along the ground."

The most amazing distinction here is that, in his creation of mankind, the Creator did not speak to the soil, the water, or the firmament. He spoke to himself, saying, "Let *us* make man in our *image*, in our *likeness*, and let them *rule* [have dominion or rulership over the rest of creation]."

Many of us miss the essential point here. Humans were not just made by God, but they were also drawn out of his own nature.

The word *"image"* used in this verse means the following in the original Hebrew text:

> *selem* (6754), "statue; image; copy."...The word...means "image" in the sense of essential nature....Human nature in its internal and external characteristics.... So, too, God made man in His own "image," reflecting some of His own perfections: perfect in knowledge, righteousness, and holiness, and with dominion over the creatures....in Gen. 1:26 (the first occurrence of the word) the "image" of God is represented by two Hebrew words (*selem* and *demut*)."[16]

HUMANS WERE NOT JUST MADE BY GOD BUT WERE DRAWN OUT OF HIS OWN NATURE.

The word for *likeness* is akin to *image* but embraces an additional meaning: "*demut* (1823), 'likeness; shape; figure; form; pattern.'...First, the word means 'pattern,' in the sense of the specifications from which an actual item is made."[17] The verb form of *likeness* is the following: "*damah* (1819), 'to be like, resemble, be or act like, liken or compare, devise, balance or ponder.'"[18]

Why is it so important to understand these words and their implications? Because these are the words that define and describe the essence of your composition, capacity, ability, potential, and value. They also confirm and reveal how the Creator designed you and why.

According to the above definitions and meanings, to be made in God's image and likeness means that you possess the spiritual nature, characteristics, essential specifications, and "substances" of God and are a reflection of his spiritual qualities. It also denotes that you were designed to be like, act like, and function like the Creator. In essence, God created you from his own substance and released you from his own Spirit, and therefore, as far as species go, you are in the "god class" in the sense that you are considered his "son" or offspring.

However, even more important than this knowledge is knowing and understanding why God the Creator chose to create you and me in this manner—reflecting his amazing qualities. The reason God did this is the key to understanding the nature of the human (leadership) spirit.

REDISCOVERING YOUR LEADERSHIP PURPOSE

Remember that everything God does is motivated by his purpose, and therefore the original purpose for a product determines its design, composition, capacity, and potential. Purpose may be defined as "original intent" or "reason for creation." For example, God created seeds to produce trees and plants, and therefore they naturally posses the inherent abilities and capacities to perform this purpose. Fish were created to swim, and thus their ability and capacity to swim is inherent in their design and instincts. They never need to attend swimming school.

Birds, on the other hand, were created for the purpose of flight and naturally come with the inherent design and ability to fulfill that purpose. Birds never attend flight school. The principle is that whatever the Creator established as the original purpose for his creation determined its natural, inherent design, its raw material, and its capacity, capability, natural talents, and potential.

This principle begs the question, "Why, then, did the Creator create mankind?" The answer is found in his declaration of his purpose and original intent for humanity: "Let them rule ["have dominion"]...over all the earth." He created us out of himself because of his intent that we rule over the earth. Again, purpose is the reason for the creation of something. In essence, it is the reason why a thing exists.

HUMAN BEINGS ARE MADE OUT OF RULERSHIP MATERIAL.

With this definition in mind, it is now critical for us to define the word *"dominion,"* for this is God's expressed purpose for the creation of mankind. The meaning of dominion in Genesis 1:26 is *radah*, which means "to tread down, i.e. subjugate; spec. to crumble off:—(come to, make to) have dominion, prevail against, reign, (bear, make to) rule."[19]

I hope that by now you are convinced that the purpose for your creation is to have rulership, dominion, mastery, authority, and leadership over the earth and its environment. However, if the Creator's purpose for your existence is leadership, rulership, and management over the earthly realm, then perhaps it might be helpful to look at a few principles of purpose as they relate to creation:

1. Purpose determines design.

2. Purpose determines potential.

3. Purpose determines natural abilities.

4. Purpose determines capacity and ability.

5. Purpose determines natural talents.

6. Purpose determines natural desires.

7. Purpose determines fulfillment and personal satisfaction.

8. Purpose is the source of passion.

9. Purpose gives existence meaning.

10. Purpose is the measure of success and failure.

Through these principles, we are again led to this vital principle: If something is created to do something, it is designed with the ability to do it. This concept is at the heart of the leadership spirit. **If we were created to be leaders, then we must all possess the capacity, inherent desire, natural talents, potential, and abilities that correspond to being a leader.** You cannot demand from a product what it does not have.

Recall what God required of humanity. The Creator expressed his intent and assignment for human beings through what he said they were to do. God wasn't speaking just to the first man, Adam, but to all humanity, because inside that one man were the seeds of all mankind. The Creator's intent was that the human creature rule and dominate both with him and for him. His intent was to share his rulership and his administration of creation with humanity.

In order to understand more about ourselves in our capacity as leaders, we must examine the nature of the Creator, since we were designed to reflect his attributes and characteristics. The Creator doesn't have dominion; he is the very essence of dominion; it is what he is. He doesn't have authority; he is the very nature of authority. He doesn't have love; he is love. He doesn't have glory; he is glory. He does not possess leadership; he is leadership. Similarly, man does not acquire dominion; he is made out of rulership material. He does not develop power; it is inherent within him. In effect, leadership is not something that man can "possess." It is part of who he is.

THE PURPOSE FOR YOUR CREATION IS TO HAVE RULERSHIP OVER THE EARTH AND ITS ENVIRONMENT.

The Creator is a leader-maker. Being designed in the image and likeness of God means that we were ordained by him to be leaders. He did not produce us and then decide that he would develop us into leaders. We were designed with that in mind. Because he created us to be leaders and dominators, he had to use leadership and dominion "material." This material originates only in him, so he made us out of his own nature.

DESIGNED TO DOMINATE

Every manufacturer designs his product with the right components, engineered to fulfill the function that the product is created to perform. In essence, the purpose of the product dictates the mechanical and engineering components required to fulfill the manufacturer's intent. Its "circuits" are right for the job.

This principle holds true for all creation, including human beings. The Creator caused to be inherent in each created entity—including the apex of his creation, mankind—everything it needs to fulfill its original purpose. The original purpose for mankind, defined and established by the Creator, was to "rule ["have dominion"]...over all the earth." Since the word *"dominion"* in this case means to reign and rule, the Creator wired all humans with the capacity and natural ability to lead.

We can conclude that human beings are wired for leadership. Humanity has the natural circuitry to have dominion over its environment. The greatest evidence of what a product can do or is capable of is determined by the demands made on it by the one who made it. Therefore, **God's requirement that we dominate is evidence that the ability to lead is inherent in every human spirit. This is *the leadership spirit.***

LEADERS BY NATURE

We are leaders by nature. Every human has the instinct for leadership, even though most of us never manifest it. The desire to lead and achieve greatness is natural, even though many of us deny that this silent, passionate longing exists in every human heart. Leadership is your desire and your destiny.

The ultimate leader, Jesus Christ, had an interesting encounter with a small group of men whom he had chosen to train as leaders. His training school lasted three years, and his success as a mentor and trainer is evidenced by the successful impact his students have had on the world and on human development over the past two thousand years. Let's listen in on one of their conversations, which he used as an opportunity to teach about the definition and precepts of true leadership.

THE LEADERSHIP SECRET TO GREATNESS

In the New Testament book of Matthew, one of Jesus's students wrote this account of a request that was made by two of his fellow students who were in the leadership training school. He recorded it like this:

> Then the mother of Zebedee's sons came to Jesus with her sons and, kneeling down, asked a favor of him. "What is it you want?" he asked. She said, "Grant that one of these two sons of mine may sit at your right and the other at your left in your kingdom." "You don't know what you are asking," Jesus said to them. "Can you drink the cup I am going to drink?" "We can," they answered. Jesus said to them, "You will indeed drink from my cup, but to sit at my right or left is not for me to grant. These places belong to those for whom they have been prepared by my Father." When the ten heard about this, they were indignant with the two brothers. Jesus called them together and said, "You know that the rulers of the Gentiles lord it over them, and their high officials exercise authority over them. Not so with you."

HUMAN BEINGS ARE WIRED FOR LEADERSHIP.

Next, Jesus made an amazing statement. Please first note that he did not rebuke the brothers for desiring to be great and seeking leadership positions. As a matter of fact, with the following statement, he went even further and showed them *how* to become great. Why did he not rebuke them? Because he knew and understood the nature and inherent passion of the human creature.

> Instead, whoever wants to become great among you must be your servant, and whoever wants to be first must be your slave—just as the Son of Man did not come to be served, but to serve, and to give his life as a ransom for many.

I believe that this story contains the greatest secret of true leadership, as well as the process necessary for becoming a genuine leader. With his answer to this question of greatness, Jesus expressed the key, the nature, and the process for you to discover and manifest your true leadership spirit.

What is natural about the leadership spirit? He said that whoever wants to be great must be the servant of all, and that he who wants to be first must be last. Therefore, the secret to greatness is in serving everyone else.

To understand this principle, you must answer the question, "What do I serve to others?" I believe that this is the greatest revelation of true leadership I have ever discovered and exceeds all the theories and research from the past. What Jesus is stating here is that, to become the great leader you were created and destined to become, you must discover your unique inherent gift and assignment (your original purpose) and serve that to the world of mankind. Do not seek greatness, but seek to serve your gift to others to the maximum extent that you can, and you will become a sought-after person.

In essence, Jesus defined true leadership as becoming a person who is valuable to others, rather than a person of just position or fame. **If you find your unique gift or special talent and commit to serving it to the world of mankind, then your significance will cause people to seek you out. You will become an influence through exercising your gift, rather than through manipulation. The more you become a person whose gift is valued, the greater your influence will be.**

Leadership means discovering and serving yourself to the world. When you do this effectively, people will call you a leader. All true leaders are simply glorified servants. Genuine leadership is not measured by how many people serve you but by how many people you serve. The greater your service, the greater your value to others, and the greater your leadership. My admonition to you is not to seek greatness but to serve your way to leadership. **The shortest distance to leadership is service.**

THE SECRET TO GREATNESS IS IN SERVING EVERYONE ELSE.

In his leadership training session on greatness, Jesus revealed his leadership attitude and used himself as an example of serving your way to leadership, saying, "The Son of Man did not come to be served, but to serve, and to give his life as a ransom for many." In other words, he was explaining what makes a person great. It was as if he was saying, "I'm an example. Study me. What is my gift? What did I come into the world to do? What is my purpose? What is my assignment?" He came to be a ransom or substitute for the many so that they might benefit from his sacrifice. Therefore, he was saying, "See? That's how you become great. I'm fulfilling my purpose. I'm serving myself to the world and giving my life for the benefit of others. I'm serving as a ransom for everybody so that they can be set free."

He is also essentially saying to us, "Find what you're supposed to do, and serve it to others. Then you'll become great." Again, this means that your leadership greatness is not in a title or a position. A person becomes a slave or servant because he exists for the people he serves. Slaves exist for their masters. In a sense, as leaders, the world becomes our "master."

Let's return to the question, "What do I serve to others?" Whatever we were created to do, God built us for. This helps us to understand that we can often tell what our leadership domain is by what we are naturally designed with. What are your inclinations, likes, passions, talents, and natural abilities? These are all part of your design. They indicate the area(s) that you are supposed to have dominion in. This becomes what is called your domain. **Find your domain and serve it to the world. Others have been waiting for your gift all your life. Therefore, lead through service.**

SERVANT LEADERSHIP

The above discussion reintroduces the greatest leadership philosophy and secret ever given to mankind and emanates from the original concept of leadership introduced in the first book written by Moses: Each person was created to dominate in a specific area of gifting. This leadership concept is called "servant leadership" and expresses the philosophy that all human beings were designed and born to serve their unique gifts and talents to the world.

This philosophy naturally implies that every human came to this planet with a seed of greatness buried in a gift needed by the world. Servant leadership, then, is the ultimate form of leadership and manifests the true nature of mankind and the image of its Creator.

EVERY HUMAN HAS A SEED OF GREATNESS BURIED IN A GIFT NEEDED BY THE WORLD.

Servant leadership integrates all of the following precepts. It is—

- the discovery of one's purpose, gift, and talent and the commitment to give them in service to mankind.

- being prepared to serve one's gift to the world at every opportunity for the betterment of humanity.

- serving oneself to the world.

- "self-distribution" to your generation.

- the maximization of self-manifestation.

- the pursuit of an inherent vision in order to serve others.

The natural results of servant leadership are the following:

- Authenticity, authority, and authorization

- Originality, from not being a copy of anyone else

- Genuine confidence, based on one's natural ability

- Personal fulfillment, stemming from satisfaction

- A sense of intrinsic value, based on the knowledge of one's significance

- No competition, because of one's uniqueness

- No comparison, because of one's distinctiveness

- No jealousy, because of one's value

- No fear, because of one's conviction

Again, servant leadership is the ultimate form of true leadership and protects the individual from the traps that entangle the power-hungry, insecure, unqualified "shadows" who parade as leaders in many of our communities. Servant leadership is about expending yourself to increase the value of others. Peter Drucker observed that all effective leaders have ensured that they themselves were "the kind of person that they wanted to be, respect, and believe in. In this way, they fortified themselves against the leader's greatest temptation—to do things that are popular rather than right and to do petty, mean, sleazy things."[20]

PRINCIPLES OF LEADERSHIP

A careful study of the lessons taught by Jesus in the above discourse will reveal the following principles of leadership:

- Leadership is predetermined and not a preference.

- Leadership is a prepared position.

- Leadership demands a price.

- Leadership is inherent.

- Leadership is a divine deposit.

- Leadership is not for you but for others.

- Leadership is becoming your true self for the benefit of others.

These principles are the foundation of true leadership and serve as the measure of leadership effectiveness.

THE ATTITUDE OF THE LEADERSHIP SPIRIT

Understanding our leadership nature is essential because the way in which we think about ourselves determines our attitudes and actions. When you discover that the Creator made you with the same nature that he has, then you understand that your desire to lead is natural. However, as we will look at more closely in the next chapter, *the leadership spirit,* our inherent natural capacity, comes with a *spirit of leadership*—an attitude.

LEADERSHIP IS BECOMING YOUR TRUE SELF FOR THE BENEFIT OF OTHERS.

When God told Adam to name the animals, for example, Adam didn't sit back and try to argue with him about it, saying, "There are too many animals. How can I name all these species?" He never hesitated. Instead, he just did it. He had the confidence, the conviction, and the authority of the spirit of leadership. It is important to note that God did not give Adam a list of animal names to choose from. Instead, he allowed Adam to draw on the capacity he had within him, in order to show him that his ability to do so already existed.

The capacity to respond to responsibility is inherent in the nature of all humans, but most of us avoid opportunities to activate or maximize it. I believe that the Creator has designed life in such a way that it constantly makes demands on our hidden leadership potential. Again, the principle is this: Whatever God calls for, he provides for.

THE NATURE OF THE LEADERSHIP SPIRIT

MANAGER OF ONE'S ENVIRONMENT

When we speak of the nature of someone or something, it has to do with what is natural to the person or thing. It expresses the concept of "inherent essence." Every created thing possesses an innate nature. It is a natural part of its existence. The nature of a thing is determined by its purpose and function, and it dictates its intrinsic instincts, gifts, and abilities. Remember our earlier example that a bird's nature is natural to its inherent purpose of flight, and its design, anatomy, and abilities are built to reflect that nature? Likewise, the nature of a fish expresses its inherent purpose.

THE LEADERSHIP SPIRIT COMES WITH A SPIRIT OF LEADERSHIP.

The nature of the leadership spirit is the inherent desire of all mankind to control and regulate both environment and circumstances. This is what we call management. This desire is natural; even when it is not our actual experience, the desire is still present. Have you ever heard one busy stay-at-home mother say to another, "How are you managing?" This is a phrase that many of us use, but we don't realize what we are saying. When a homemaker asks her neighbor this question, she is really inquiring, "How are you handling your circumstances?" This is a normal question of one leader to another. So you have a homemaker, who may not even know that she is a leader, naturally wanting to manage her children, her budget, the environment of the house, and so on. That desire comes from the leadership nature within her.

Even though people may ignore their inherent nature or may be denied the full exercise of it, the desire to control and manage one's own destiny still resides deep in the heart of the human spirit. It is our natural desire to lead.

EXERTER OF INFLUENCE

It is also the nature of leadership to influence. All people naturally want to influence the world around them. When you think about it, everyone is in the influence game—whether it's a salesperson trying to influence a prospective client, a child trying to influence a parent, or a young man trying to influence a young woman. Everyone desires to influence because we naturally want to be in control. Yet we've confused influence with domination. According to the original design, we're not supposed to dominate other people but to have dominion over the earth and its resources. When we don't understand this distinction, we manipulate and abuse others and frustrate the expression of their own God-given leadership nature. Exerting proper influence means inspiring others through the leadership gift that we have been given. The true nature of leadership is the attraction of others to our gifts, which are deployed in their service.

COMFORTABLE WITH POWER

Another aspect of the leadership spirit is that it is comfortable with power. Power, in itself, is natural for the human spirit. Again, problems arise when we distort our natural gifts.

For example, when a person doesn't have a good self-concept, a strong self-worth, and high self-esteem, he will use his power in negative ways in order to compensate for his feelings of inferiority and vulnerability. He will intimidate, manipulate, and oppress.

EVERYONE DESIRES INFLUENCE; HOWEVER, WE'VE CONFUSED INFLUENCE WITH DOMINANCE.

When you realize this truth, it helps you to understand why many people act the way they do. This is the reason tyrants tyrannize. Have you ever noticed that when some people come into positions of power, their personalities seem to change for the worse? They are tasting the nature of leadership, but they don't have the character to manage it—or themselves—well. This is the source of many of the problems we are seeing in the contemporary business world, as well as in national politics.

We all naturally seek power. The homeless man sleeping under a bridge in a cardboard box desires power just as much as the man who is sleeping in a twelve-bedroom house by a lake. We use a thousand different ways to try to gain power, such as—

- positions of influence
- money
- association and membership in influential or elite groups
- material status symbols, such as clothing, houses, cars, and jets
- status in society, such as living in a certain neighborhood or region

- educational achievements
- type of jobs or careers

Again, the desire for power, in itself, isn't wrong. It's our attitude toward and use of power that can be harmful. If we don't desire power of some sort, our natural inclination has been altered by oppression, apathy, fear, or other things. I think that we need to admit to our desire for power before we can become friendly with it. If we deny our penchant for it, we deceive ourselves as well as others.

Many people desire to be successful in their work so that they can get the revenue that their companies have promised them, so that they can generate more business, so that they can gain more money, so that they can buy more things, so that they can achieve a better standard of living, so that they can feel important and influential, so that they can do or buy whatever they want. The principal objective is power—power to control their standard of life and circumstances.

Gaining wealth, in itself, is not a bad thing, even though many people have been taught to think that it is. The problem is how some people go about gaining it and the attitude that they have toward it. According to the first book written by Moses, God told Abraham, the Father of the Jewish people, in effect, "I'm going to bless you and make you a blessing." Abraham became the richest man in his region. Why would God want to make him rich? In order to give him influence. Abraham was very comfortable with the power that he had. He was not proud but was grateful for it and responsible with it. He had influence with others, and he credited that influence to God.

Why would God, therefore, want to cause a person to be rich? In order to give him influence. Moses, in his book of Deuteronomy, stated these words to the people of Israel: "Remember the LORD your God, for it is he who gives you the ability to produce wealth." It is important to note that the biblical exhortations concerning money and wealth (for example, "The love of money is a root of all kinds of evil") do not warn against possessing money or wealth but rather against allowing money and wealth to possess us. **Loving money at the expense of the dignity, value, and welfare of others is an abuse of our power to get wealth.**

THE DESIRE FOR POWER, IN ITSELF, ISN'T WRONG.

The desire for power to control circumstances is one of the most potent motivating factors of human behavior. Again, when the young Jewish rabbi Jesus began training his leadership team, one of the first things he did was to give them power—power to exorcise demons, heal the sick, raise the dead, and so forth. He sent them out, and they went and started using that power. When they returned, they told him everything they had done, and they started celebrating. The biblical account says, "In that hour Jesus rejoiced."

Why would Jesus give a group of men, which included fishermen, a tax collector, and a zealot, that much power? He gave them power so that they could taste how it felt to put their inherent leadership nature to use in a positive way, and they came back excited about it. Then he got excited about their excitement because he saw humanity exercising power in the way the Creator first intended them to. Mankind was in control of his circumstances. Imagine a fisherman having power over death, cleansing lepers, opening blind eyes, and unstopping deaf ears.

I believe that this early experience is one reason why his disciples left their businesses and their jobs and never returned to them. They followed Jesus because, when they were with him, they tasted their true selves. He introduced them to themselves. He reconnected them to who they really were. He tapped into their inherent leadership nature and potential. If you study the lessons he taught, they all relate to this theme. He walked on the water and said, in effect, "You can do this; come." He healed the sick, and then he said, "Go ahead, do it." He was showing them how to have dominion over their environment, how to have power over circumstances through the power of God.

Earlier, I mentioned the request of the mother of James and John that they have leadership positions in Jesus's kingdom government: "May my sons sit on your right and your left in your kingdom?" Again, it is important to note that he did not rebuke them or deny their request to become great. On the contrary, he went on to teach them how to achieve greatness.

I think that we sometimes miss his point. He said, in essence, "The rulers of this world lord it over people, but that is not what you are to do. He who wants to become great among you must be a servant." He didn't say, "Don't try to be great because that's prideful." He didn't tell them that their desire was wrong. Instead, he told them how to get there, what it means to become a great leader.

We should remember that James and John became two of Jesus's favorites. I believe that this was because they had the right interests, the right pursuits, and the right attitudes. They didn't want to be average. They didn't want to be followers.

When someone comes to us and says that he wants to do something great and big, we normally think that he is overly ambitious and proud. Actually, he's exercising his true nature. But what do we do? We intimidate him in order to try to discourage him. Sometimes, we even use religion as a justification for telling others not to seek greatness. But here Jesus is telling his disciples, in essence, "You want to be great? Then here's how to do it: You serve others."

Loving money at the expense of others is an abuse of our power to get wealth.

Likewise, the early church writer Paul wrote in his first epistle to his associate Timothy, "If anyone sets his heart on being an overseer, he desires a noble task." Paul was saying, "Look, if you want to be a great person, if you want to be a leader, that's not bad." We've been taught that this desire is bad, yet Paul simply went on to explain what is required for leadership. Please note that the apostle emphasized that the *desire* to be a leader (setting one's heart on it) is "noble." I want you to truly understand that the human desire for greatness is natural and inherent.

Finding Your "Mansion"— Your Position of Authority

In a number of ways, Jesus Christ introduced his disciples to the phenomenon of the power that a human being can have. In the gospel account written by one of the young rabbi's disciples named John, it is recorded that when Jesus began to explain the necessity for his departure from the earth and his to return to heaven, his disciple-students became nervous and depressed. To alleviate their fears, he offered them this comfort: "Let not your heart be troubled; you believe in God, believe also in Me. In My Father's house are many mansions; if it were not so, I would have told you. I go to prepare a place for you." This statement is critical to our understanding of our human nature and to our recognition that God knows our inherent need for leadership.

A casual reading and interpretation of this passage through the filter of Western culture usually leads to the conclusion that Jesus was promising a physical house, in particular, a structure that resembles the large dwelling we call a mansion. However, it is important to understand that there is no reference in the Bible to an actual physical structure in heaven in which we will live. Therefore, the word in the original language must have a different meaning.

A careful study of the Greek word *mone*, translated "mansion" or "dwelling place," indicates a position or place of residing or abiding:

> *mone* (3438), primarily "a staying, abiding" (akin to *meno*, "to abide"), denotes an "abode" (Eng., "manor," "manse," etc.), translated "mansions" in John 14:2; "abode" in v. 23. There is nothing in the word to indicate separate compartments in heaven; neither does it suggest temporary resting places on the road.[21]

I believe that Jesus was referring to the permanent restoration of our spiritual standing or position with God, which also reestablished our place of authority and power on the Earth, which the Creator had given us.

The concept of a place of authority was also used by Jesus when the two disciples asked him about greatness and leadership positions in His kingdom, and he replied, "To sit at my right or left is not for me to grant. These places [positions of authority or places of authority] belong to those for whom they have been prepared by my Father." The Greek word for "sit" is *kathizo*, meaning "to seat down, i.e. set (fig. appoint)."[22]

"Let not your heart be troubled....In My Father's House are many mansions."

A similar concept occurs in the biblical book of Jude, in which the author talks about positions of authority given by God to angels who subsequently abandoned them. The various translations below indicate that they left a place of authority and use imagery similar to "mansions," including "home," "abode," and "habitation."

> And the angels who did not keep their **positions of authority** but abandoned their own **home**—these he has kept in darkness, bound with everlasting chains for judgment on the great Day. (NIV, emphasis added)

> And angels who did not keep their own **domain**, but abandoned their proper **abode**, He has kept in eternal bonds under darkness for the judgment of the great day. (NASB, emphasis added)

> And the angels which kept not their first **estate**, but left their own **habitation**, he hath reserved in everlasting

chains under darkness unto the judgment of the great
day.   (KJV, emphasis added)

And angels that kept not their own **principality**, but
left their proper **habitation**, he hath kept in everlasting
bonds under darkness unto the judgment of the great
day.   (ASV, emphasis added)

After Jesus said, "In My Father's house are many mansions," he went on to say, "If it were not so, I would have told
you." In other words, there is a position of leadership, of power,
for everybody. It is interesting and important to note that the
comfort Jesus offered his distressed and depressed disciples
was that each one of them would be restored to a relationship
with God the Father that included a position of leadership
and authority. He told them that his departure was necessary
to secure these positions.

Perhaps this assurance was given in order to confirm
that that ultimate purpose and goal of the redemptive work
of God through Jesus Christ was to restore all of humanity to
its position of rule and dominion on the Earth—its leadership
authority. Perhaps this is also why the final promise of Jesus
to his followers just before his ascension was, "You will receive
power"—an enablement to impact, change, and control circumstances. He promised to provide what he knew we wanted
and needed, as well as what was natural for the apex of God's
creation.

THE ATTRIBUTES OF THE LEADERSHIP SPIRIT

When we talk about the attributes of leadership, we are
referring to the manifest qualities that reflect the natural source
and nature of our Creator. According to *Merriam-Webster's 11th*

Collegiate Dictionary, the word *attribute* comes from a Latin word meaning "to bestow." The Creator has bestowed on us the attributes of a leadership spirit. Here are some of the definitions of *attribute*: "an inherent characteristic," "an object closely associated with or belonging to a specific person, thing, or office," and "a word ascribing a quality."

THERE IS A POSITION OF LEADERSHIP, OF POWER, FOR EVERYBODY.

Once more, since God is our Creator and the "material" from which we were created, then in order to understand our leadership attributes, it is naturally imperative for us to explore, study, and come to understand the nature of His attributes. In essence, if you want to know and understand yourself, your nature, and your abilities, it is necessary for you to know God, who is your Source.

OMNIPOTENCE

The first attribute of God is that he is omnipotent or all-powerful. How do we apply this attribute to ourselves? Omnipotence means "all-inherent power." It can also be described as a sense of secure ability in pursuing and fulfilling one's purpose and will. Since we were made in the image and likeness of the Creator, and possess that same ability in a measure, this means that we inherently have power that enables us to accomplish what we were created to do.

In addition, power can be defined as the proper use of energy. The application for us is this: God does not use energy in a negative way. His power is creative. A true leader who has tapped into his essential nature uses power to create things, to make things better for people, just as God does. The Creator uses his power to produce what is good, and we are meant to do the same.

OMNISCIENCE

The Creator is also omniscient or all-knowing. Because we have his nature, we have the facility to understand and retain knowledge. I believe that we are capable of learning as much as we want to. In this sense, our ability to learn is infinite. Moreover, we can never grow too old to learn. We have the capacity to know more than we think we can.

This means that whatever you've learned so far is not enough for you to know. Our ability to know is inherent, and any perceived limitation of this ability is based on our conclusion that we've learned all that we can or want to know. Yet this is not all that we are *able* to know. We have a long way to go in order to match our potential for knowledge.

Paul of Tarsus said that a day will come when we will meet our Creator face-to-face, and then we will "know as we are known." We can begin that process now. For example, although I can't bodily go into the heavenlies to communicate with and learn from God, I have the capacity to do this in my spirit. We need to be more aware of our ability to know our Creator and the world that he has made.

OMNIPRESENCE

The third attribute of God is that he is omnipresent. This means that he is everywhere and that there is no place in heaven, the universe, or on earth that threatens or intimidates him. Here is how I apply this attribute to our leadership spirit: When you read about the life of Jesus, you sense that he could be anywhere and be comfortable. He was equally at ease in the presence of high officials, the poor, his family, his disciples, and anyone else he met. A true leader has the capacity to adapt to and function among any group of people effectively.

IF YOU WANT TO KNOW AND UNDERSTAND YOURSELF, YOU MUST KNOW GOD.

In addition, as I said earlier, you can put a natural leader anywhere on earth, and in a matter of time, he is in charge of his environment. His environment doesn't control him; he controls it. Again, because we are made in the image of our Creator, we have the ability to dominate our environments. We can control and govern them instead of becoming victims of them. But we have to first discover that we have this ability because of the Source from which we came.

INTEGRITY

The fourth attribute of God is his absolute integrity. This means that he is always pure in his motives and intentions. In essence, God is always and completely integrated or one with himself. His intent, words, and actions are one with himself. This is also the concept of being holy. It means that what he says, what he does, and who he is are one and the same. In God, there is no contradiction. True leaders are honest. There is no manipulation or deception in their dealings with others or their pursuit of their visions. True leaders possess candor and sense of self. They are true to themselves first and then to others.

RECONNECTING WITH THE LEADERSHIP SPIRIT

THE SPIRIT OF LEADERSHIP IS A SPIRIT THAT IS COMFORTABLE IN THE CREATOR'S COMPANY

When we understand that man was created in God's image, likeness, and nature and possesses his essence and characteristics, then it should be obvious that, in order for man to understand himself and his true potential, abilities, and nature, he must reconnect to his Source, the Creator. **The leadership spirit is the essence of the spirit-man, who can comprehend his identity only from relating to his Source.** This relationship should be natural and mutually fulfilling. God and man belong together, and therefore the presence of God is man's natural and ideal environment.

WE CAN GOVERN OUR ENVIRONMENTS INSTEAD OF BECOMING VICTIMS OF THEM.

True leaders are born in the presence of their Creator because that is where they discover the truth about themselves. Just as the life hidden within a seed is brought forth when the seed is placed in the right environment of the soil, the true potential of humanity germinates when it is in the presence of God. To discover the truth about your ability and destiny, you must rediscover the value of a relationship with your Source.

The first man, Adam, was created in God's presence and enjoyed spiritual relationship with his Creator as a natural experience, not as a "religious" one. Adam didn't have to try to get into God's presence. He didn't need to perform sophisticated religious customs or rituals. In the first book written by Moses, it is recorded that Adam "walked and talked with God in the cool of the day."

TRUE LEADERS ARE HONEST; THERE IS NO MANIPULATION OR DECEPTION IN THEM.

Adam was comfortable in God's company because he was just like him. In effect, the nature of the leadership spirit is to be comfortable in the presence of power, authority, and might without being intimidated. When the leadership spirit is fully restored, you revere and respect God and his authority but are never fearful in his presence; you rejoice in his company. **True leaders respect and honor authority but are comfortable in its presence.**

THE SPIRIT OF LEADERSHIP IS AN OTHERWORLDLY CONFIDENCE

The restoration of the leadership spirit also brings a level of confidence that is not common, and that, in the eyes of many, seems to come from another world. Your thinking and perception come from a higher plane. When Jesus was on trial before the Roman procurator Pilate, the ruler asked him, "Are you a king?" He answered, "My kingdom is not of this world." In other words, "My government is from another place." When a person rediscovers the leadership spirit, his confidence emerges from an understanding of who and what he is and an awareness of his true capacity and abilities. This natural confidence, grounded in a conviction of self-discovery and self-awareness, is so sure that it is sometimes mistaken for arrogance by the insecure.

THE LEADERSHIP SPIRIT

THE SPIRIT OF LEADERSHIP DEMONSTRATES INTERNAL SOUNDNESS AND SECURITY

When you rediscover the leadership spirit, you love and are comfortable with yourself because you become aware that your self-worth, self-esteem, and self-concept are the result of the fact that you were made in God's image and possess his qualities and characteristics. Suddenly, you're not trying to compensate for a sense of inadequacy or inferiority, and you're not trying to use or abuse people to make yourself feel superior.

The self-esteem derived from self-discovery sets you free from the assessments of others. When the estimation of your personal value and worth is found in your realization that you are in the "god-class," in the sense of your being created in God's image and likeness (though not *equal* to him), then the result is a high self-esteem. This high self-esteem sets you free from the negative effects of other people's opinions. That is the reason that you can serve them as a servant leader. Even if they mistreat you, it doesn't affect your estimation of your value to them. This is why Jesus Christ could say on the cross, "Father, forgive them, for they do not know what they are doing." He knew how valuable he was to them—both in who he was and in what he was doing on their behalf. His self-esteem was intact, right to the end.

Because a true leadership spirit is borne out of a strong sense of self-worth and self-esteem, leaders can be compassionate, patient, forgiving, and kind. They do not need to gain their self-assessment from the people whom they are serving. They understand that you cannot set people free until you are free from them. If you need the people whom you are leading in order to feel important, then you cannot lead them. Ultimately, they will end up leading you.

This is why discovering the leadership spirit is a prerequisite to serving. If you never discover who you are, you will always misinterpret the attitudes and actions of others. You'll also underestimate everyone else—you'll consider them less than what they really are because you'll want to feel that you are above them. You will "under-esteem" them. However, you will treat people well and esteem them highly when you rediscover the leadership spirit and are secure in yourself.

THE LEADERSHIP SPIRIT POSSESSES A NATURAL LOVE FOR ALL HUMAN BEINGS

Self-discovery is at the heart of the leadership spirit. It is birthed from rediscovering your true nature, potential, capacity, character, and abilities through rediscovering your Source—God. **This will naturally lead you to the revelation that all humans are created in God's image and likeness, and therefore possess the same value, worth, and estimation as yourself.**

SELF-ESTEEM DERIVED FROM SELF-DISCOVERY SETS YOU FREE FROM THE ASSESSMENTS OF OTHERS.

If each individual bears the same image of God that you do, then it becomes impossible to separate his image in man from himself. In essence, it is not possible to say that you love God but hate mankind, for this becomes a contradiction. You will have a natural love for others because you will perceive that you and they are essentially the same.

Since they are made in God's image and likeness, as you are, then any negative approach or act against them is an act against yourself and against the Creator, as well. A true leader who is reconnected with the leadership spirit understands that serving mankind is serving God himself, and thus serves his fellowmen from a motivation of love and respect.

IT IS NOT POSSIBLE TO LOVE GOD BUT HATE MANKIND.

We see this principle in the following expressions spoken by Jesus:

> Whoever does not love does not know God, because God is love.

> If anyone says, "I love God," yet hates his brother, he is a liar. For anyone who does not love his brother, whom he has seen, cannot love God, whom he has not seen. And he has given us this command: Whoever loves God must also love his brother.

> Jesus replied: "'Love the Lord your God with all your heart and with all your soul and with all your mind.' This is the first and greatest commandment. And the second is like it: 'Love your neighbor as yourself.' All the Law and the Prophets hang on these two commandments."

The above texts clearly indicate that love for mankind is a priority and is evidence that one loves God, the Creator of humanity. Perhaps this is the major ingredient missing in leadership today. The focus is on results and performance more than on values, such as love, caring, compassion, and kindness. We need leaders who love their followers more than they love their goals and objectives. We must understand and capture this spirit of leadership in order to fully manifest the leadership potential hidden within each of us.

CHAPTER PRINCIPLES

1. To exercise leadership, you must believe that you are inherently a leader.

2. The *leadership spirit* is the inherent leadership capacity and potential that is the essential nature of human beings. The *spirit of leadership* is the mind-set or attitudes that accompany a true leadership spirit and allow the dormant leadership potential to be fully manifested and maximized.

3. Trapped within every follower is a hidden leader.

4. Our leadership capacity is buried under social, cultural, and ideological perceptions that restrict, discourage, and hinder its manifestation.

5. The leadership spirit is the intrinsic capacity of the human spirit to lead, manage, and dominate, which was placed there at the point of creation and made necessary by the purpose and assignment for which man was created.

6. Leadership is not something that human beings have to strive for; it is something that is inherent within us because of our purpose and design.

7. When we become our true selves, we will naturally be leaders.

8. If something is created to do something, it is designed with the ability to do it.

9. Humanity was designed with the natural components or "circuitry" to dominate its environment.

10. God's requirement that we dominate is evidence that the ability to lead is inherent in every human spirit.

11. The secret to leadership greatness is in serving others. To become the great leader that you were created and destined to become, you must discover your unique inherent gift and assignment (your original purpose) and serve that to the world of mankind.

12. The principles of leadership are (1) leadership is predetermined and not a preference; (2) leadership is a prepared position; (3) leadership demands a price; (4) leadership is inherent; (5) leadership is a divine deposit; (6) leadership is not for you but for others; (7) leadership is becoming your true self for the benefit of others.

13. The nature of the leadership spirit includes the following: (1) manager of one's environment; (2) exerter of influence; and (3) comfortable with power.

14. When Jesus said, "In my Father's house, there are many mansions," he was referring to the permanent restoration of our spiritual standing or position with God, which also reestablished our place of authority and power on the Earth.

15. Four essential attributes of the Creator—as well as the leadership spirit—are (1) omnipotence, (2) omniscience, (3) omnipresence, and (4) integrity.

16. The leadership spirit is the essence of the spirit-man, who can comprehend his identity only from relating to his Source.

17. Signs of reconnection with the leadership spirit are (1) a comfortableness in the Creator's company, (2) an otherworldly confidence, (3) an internal soundness and security, and (4) a natural love for all human beings.

CHAPTER FOUR
THE SPIRIT OF LEADERSHIP

True leadership is not a method, a technique,
or a science but an attitude.

B y now we understand that the leadership spirit refers to the inherent spirit of mankind that possesses the natural qualities and characteristics of the Creator. Every human being possesses this spirit, but very few ever discover this truth and fewer still are aware it can be manifested.

Having the *leadership spirit* means that you are naturally created to lead. However, the *spirit of leadership* is essentially different in that it refers to the attitudes, mentality, and mind-set necessary for the leadership spirit to be manifested. Without the spirit of leadership, the leadership spirit will remain dormant.

Having the spirit of leadership means that you understand and demonstrate the mind-set of a leader. Even though you are naturally a leader, there are some things that you need to discover and develop in order to operate as a leader. **You have to choose to fulfill your leadership nature.** Having the leadership spirit without the spirit of leadership is like having a powerful automobile without the knowledge or ability to drive it. It is like a seed that never becomes the tree it was destined to be.

Let me emphasize again that no one can "teach" you to be a leader. For example, you can't train an orange to be an orange. It just naturally is one. Likewise, it is instinctive for a fish to swim. You can't teach it to move its fins and tail; it just does those things naturally.

YOU HAVE TO CHOOSE TO MANIFEST YOUR LEADERSHIP NATURE.

At some point, a mother bird will nudge her baby birds out of the nest, as if to say, "You need to do what you were naturally born to do," and they will either start flying or risk falling out of the nest. The same is true for you in the sense that you are naturally a leader. You can "fly" when you tap into what you were born to do. **Manifesting the spirit of leadership is a matter of discovering and nurturing your true self so that you naturally evidence your leadership nature.**

Sometimes we think, "If someone tells me that I'm a leader, then, okay, I'm a leader." No, you *are* a leader. The first issue is whether or not you will discover this truth for yourself. The second issue is whether you will manifest who you really are. The purpose of this book is to give you two things: the information to discover your leadership nature and the revelation of what it means to develop and live out your leadership potential. I desire to help you capture the spirit of leadership in order to ignite the leadership spirit that I know is within you.

THE SPIRIT OF LEADERSHIP

The lion who lived on the farm was always a lion, but because he grew up in an environment that was unnatural to him, he thought he was a sheep. Our environment (for example, our education, social training, cultures, nations, or families) has been defining us and giving us the parameters of what we can and can't be. The only way to counter this unnatural information is to discover our true selves by seeing a picture of our leadership nature so that we can know who we really are. Once the young lion saw the older lion, he knew what he was supposed to become. My goal for this book is to give you a picture of your true self so that you can start on the journey to fulfilling it.

DEFINING THE SPIRIT OF LEADERSHIP

There is nothing on earth as powerful as a thought or an idea. We are what we think, and we become what we continue to think. **You cannot rise above the plane of your mental conditioning. To change your life, you must change your mind.**

WE ARE WHAT WE THINK, AND WE BECOME WHAT WE CONTINUE TO THINK.

The spirit of leadership is a derivative of the leadership spirit. It is the state of mind or attitude that emanates from the nature of a leader. We'll discuss why most of us don't exhibit this state of mind in the next chapter. For now, let's look at the spirit of leadership from various definitions and perspectives that will help us to grasp this vital concept. The spirit of leadership—

- is a mind-set.

- dictates one's motivation.

- is revealed in one's response to one's environment.

- is a perception of oneself and the world.

- is the convictions that regulate one's thoughts about oneself and one's world.

- is one's personal, private philosophy of life.

- is one's thoughts about oneself and one's environment.

- is one's belief system, which controls one's behavior.

- is the source of one's actions, which determines the response of the environment. (In other words, your attitude determines how other people treat you and how the world responds to you.)

- is how you interpret the world.

- is your mental conditioning.

THE SOURCE OF OUR THOUGHTS

As I stated above, there is nothing as powerful as a thought or idea, but there is nothing more important than the *source* of our thoughts. Our thoughts are products of what we have heard or learned. What we derive our thoughts from determines the kind of thoughts we conceive and who we eventually become. If "as a person thinks in his heart, so is he," then the source from which man gets the thoughts that he thinks is most critical.

Therefore, as we approach this delicate subject of the spirit of leadership, which is essentially the thought-life of the individual, we must carefully consider the process by which thoughts transfer to our lives. The process involves the following:

1. A source transmits its ideas through words or images.

2. Words heard or images seen transmit thoughts and ideas to our minds.

3. Thoughts conceived become ideas.

4. Ideas conceived become ideologies.

5. Ideologies conceived become beliefs.

6. Beliefs conceived become convictions.

7. Convictions conceived become philosophies.

8. Philosophies conceived become lifestyles.

9. Lifestyles determine our destinies.

A careful study of the above process reveals that the most important component is the source of our thoughts. As a result, our mind-sets, attitudes, beliefs, and convictions are generally determined by someone else's ideas. It is remarkable that you and I can be living what other people *think*. Therefore, the key to living effectively is receiving your thoughts from the correct source.

When your philosophy, beliefs, thoughts, and convictions are based on the way you were created to think, you will naturally rule over your environment and fulfill your life's purpose. When they are based on erroneous thinking and attitudes, you will feel frustrated and trapped by your circumstances. This is, unfortunately, the case for many of us. That is why I often say that there is a leader trapped in every follower.

Again, the spirit of leadership refers to the mind-set or attitude of a leader. Most of the approximately seven billion people on Earth will never discover or manifest the leadership spirit hidden within them because they do not possess the correct attitudes and mind-set that they need in order to be set free and soar to their highest potential intended by the Creator. Your mind matters, and it controls how you manage matter. If you truly understand what it means to be made in the likeness of your Creator, then you will have certain attitudes toward yourself that will allow you to fulfill your leadership potential.

YOUR MIND MATTERS, AND IT CONTROLS HOW YOU MANAGE MATTER.

Let's look at how our thinking influences who we believe we are and what we believe we are able to do. We're going to build on many of the concepts that we have looked at in previous chapters.

CREATION AND SELF-CONCEPT

The first thing to consider regarding the source of our thoughts is the relationship between creation and self-concept. Your attitudes are largely a result of your self-concept—the picture you have of yourself. What is your idea about who and what you are? Your answer to this question is crucial because your self-perception influences whether or not you will realize your inherent leadership potential.

The Creator designed you in his image, and therefore he wants you to have a concept of yourself that is in line with who he is. That is the picture you are meant to have of yourself. Families pass down certain genes and traits from one generation to another. Similarly, our Father God passed along his nature to us, and that "family resemblance" is meant to be a reminder of where we come from, to whom we belong, and what we are intended to be.

Recall that the *first* thing the Creator gave his creation was not dominion but his nature. **Our self-concept and self-image are the first reality that must be established in our minds and hearts before we can effectively fulfill our purpose and become the leaders we were created to be.** If a person has power but does not possess a sound self-concept or self-image, then he or she will relate to others from that distorted perspective. As we saw in the previous chapter, this insecurity will manifest itself in fear, suspicion, distrust, and hatred of self and others.

A poor self-image or self-concept will always result in a low valuation of humanity, and it becomes the source of abuse, corruption, oppression, and the need to dominate and control others. Again, this is why it is so important to note and understand that the first thing God gave humanity in the process of creation was not power, authority, or dominion. The first installation in the creation of the mankind was an *image*—the image of God.

So God didn't give human beings power first. He gave them a self-picture. If you love yourself in the true sense, you'll always use your power to help other people rather than to harm them. How you see yourself is how you will see everyone else you relate to. You will see all men through your own self-picture. The foundation of leadership is a sound self-image.

CREATION AND SELF-WORTH

To a large degree, your thoughts and feelings about yourself are determined by your self-worth. Your self-worth is the value you place on yourself. How much value do you think you have? Again, to find the true answer, you have to go back to the beginning. The Creator made you in his image and likeness, and therefore your value is a reflection of his value. Moreover, leaders value others as they value themselves.

The majority of the people in the world do not have self-worth but "others-worth." This is the acceptance of the worth others place on you. You will never become the leader you were created to be until you become free from other people's valuation of you and perception of your worth.

GOD FIRST GAVE HUMAN BEINGS A SELF-PICTURE, NOT POWER.

The opposite of self is other. Many people spend their lives trying to appease, satisfy, and fulfill other people's appraisals of them. This is why they never become true leaders.

The essence of leadership is that you give *other* people value. In other words, you give them something valuable to contribute to and become involved in. **True leadership gives people a cause, a reason for living, and a sense of significance that gives meaning to their lives so that they feel necessary and purposeful. It gives them an outlet for expressing their own gifting. You cannot give significance if you don't already have it. You cannot lead people where you have not gone yourself.**

THE IMPACT OF INTRAPERSONAL ATTITUDE ON INTERPERSONAL ATTITUDE

Often, whatever you believe about yourself, you will believe about other people. In the fifth and last book by Moses, we find these words: "Love the LORD your God with all your heart and with all your soul and with all your strength." Jesus Christ, the ultimate leader, repeated this statement when he was asked, in effect, "What is the most important duty of all mankind?" He replied that the command to love God is the first and greatest commandment, and that the second is exactly like it: "Love your neighbor as yourself."

We've missed the fact that this is a leadership statement. If you consider his words carefully, he wasn't telling us to love our neighbors first. He was saying, in effect, that we have to love ourselves first because we can love our neighbors only to the degree that we love ourselves.

YOU CANNOT GIVE SIGNIFICANCE IF YOU DON'T ALREADY HAVE IT.

Therefore, a healthy intrapersonal relationship is a prerequisite for effective interpersonal relationships. Your attitude toward me is a reflection of your attitude toward yourself. This means that if we don't get our attitudes toward ourselves right, then we're going to have the wrong attitudes when interacting with others. It is imperative that leaders possess a healthy, wholesome love for themselves first in order to lead others effectively.

The command to "Love the LORD your God with all your heart and with all your soul and with all your strength" has to do with discovering the nature of the Creator. If you are pursuing God with everything you have, then you will discover both him and yourself. As I mentioned earlier, when this happens, you will come to the realization that everyone else on earth is made in God's image, just as you are, and therefore they possess the same value, worth, and estimation. When I love others, I am loving myself and God because we all have the same nature.

John, the first-century writer and disciple of Jesus, wrote these words over two thousand years ago: "If anyone says, 'I love God,' yet hates his brother, he is a liar." It is impossible to love the Creator and, at the same time, hate those who have been made in his image and likeness. Any negative feeling toward another human is an indication of self-hatred. Leaders must first fall in love with themselves; then they can genuinely care about those they lead. You cannot love beyond your self-love.

CREATION AND SELF-ESTEEM

While self-worth asks, "How much value do I believe I have?" self-esteem asks, "What does this mean to my environment?" Self-esteem is your estimation of your value to the world. It is how you regard yourself in terms of your contribution and usefulness to others. Self-esteem is therefore your sense of significance to the world and the universe.

Many people suffer from very low self-esteem. I have found that women are more vulnerable to low self-esteem than men are because they are more emotional by design. They have a natural and valuable gift of empathy that can backfire if they don't know who they were created to be. Many women allow men to control them because they are looking for their esteem from their relationships with males rather than from their relationship with their Creator. This is a serious problem for many women, and it hinders the expression of their leadership nature.

Again, self-esteem is your awareness of your value to your environment. After God gave human beings their self-concept and self-worth, his next instruction was for them to have dominion over the earth because he wanted them to understand how important they were to the entire environment. He esteemed them highly by making them corulers over creation.

SELF-ESTEEM IS YOUR AWARENESS OF YOUR VALUE TO YOUR ENVIRONMENT.

The Creator was showing them that he made them more important than the plants, animals, birds, and fish. A popular belief today is that human beings evolved from the animal kingdom, yet God not only distinguished us from animals by giving us his own nature but also by placing us in authority over them. Our self-esteem should be equal to the esteem with which the Creator regards us. He esteemed us so much that he gave us the ability to govern over creation, making us coleaders and corulers with him on Earth.

Our disposition toward ourselves and the world comes from our self-estimation. Our self-estimation, in turn, comes from our awareness of our value to our world. This is where we get our sense of significance and contribution in life. Now that I understand that I have been created to be a leader, I esteem myself very necessary to the world. You need to do the same thing because your leadership will come from that awareness. You must come to the point where you are convinced and convicted that you and your gift are necessary. True leaders believe that they are needed by their generation and the world.

CREATION AND SELF-AWARENESS

The greatest discovery in human experience is self-discovery. Your leadership attitude comes alive when you become aware of your true nature. The great Greek philosopher Socrates made "Know thyself" the guiding principle of his life, and this idea was perpetuated by his disciple, Plato. Yet "Know thyself" is an incomplete idea because all they knew was that there was something to learning about yourself. They didn't fully understand or explain how to do this. The only way to know yourself is to know where you originated because you are just like the Source from which you came. This is why the best way to discover and understand yourself is to discover and study the nature and attributes of God.

Needing to know God doesn't have to do with "religion" or some of the things people do in the name of religion. It has to do with being introduced to your true self. Only your Source can give you an understanding of who you are since you have the same nature and essence that he does. Knowing God leads to humanity's greatest knowledge about itself.

When a person gets to know his Creator, and finally comes to know himself, then his leadership is born. When he makes this discovery, his attitudes are adjusted. His beliefs about himself, mankind, and his role in the world are radically transformed.

DISCOVERING THE HEART OF LEADERSHIP

Your entire life is controlled and determined by your heart. Whatever is in your heart dictates your experience in life. When I mention the heart, I assume that most people immediately think of the physical organ that beats in our chests. But this is not what this word means in the context of leadership.

The Bible provides us with many truths about the heart. When it uses this word, it's usually referring to our subconscious minds and their contents. The historically renowned psychologist, Freud, in his attempt to describe and define this concept of the heart, referred to it as the "psyche." But what is the heart?

WHEN A PERSON KNOWS HIS CREATOR AND HIMSELF, THEN HIS LEADERSHIP IS BORN.

From early medieval times, the heart has been a metaphor for the center of our being. Dr. David Allen, a leading psychologist, in his book, *Contemplation,* says it this way: "It is the decision-making center where all of our choices—good and evil—are decided....The heart is both conscious and unconscious....[It] is also a place of understanding and reasoning. According to Pascal, 'The heart has reasons the mind knows not of.'...The heart is the deepest psychological ground of our personality."[23]

The heart is the seat of our reasoning, the storehouse of all our thoughts, the seedbed for our ideas, and the center of our decision making. It is the "hard drive" for our conscious minds. Our hearts or subconscious minds are what motivate us in our attitudes and actions, even though we may not be aware of what is influencing us.

Jesus, the ultimate leader of leaders, gave much attention to this aspect of the human development and training process. He emphasized the following statements to his leadership trainees:

> For out of the overflow of the heart the mouth speaks. The good man brings good things out of the good stored up in him, and the evil man brings evil things out of the evil stored up in him.

> But the things that come out of the mouth come from the heart, and these make a man "unclean." For out of the heart come evil thoughts, murder, adultery, sexual immorality, theft, false testimony, slander. These are what make a man "unclean"; but eating with unwashed hands does not make him "unclean."

> The good man brings good things out of the good stored up in his heart, and the evil man brings evil things out of the evil stored up in his heart. For out of the overflow of his heart his mouth speaks.

In these simple statements, the principle of the heart and its power to control all of one's life is evident. According to Jesus, all our actions are motivated by the content of our hearts or what is stored in our subconscious minds. Have you noticed that people's true attitudes and beliefs are often manifested when they are under pressure? They are revealing what is in their hearts.

Here are some examples of the use of the word *heart* in the Bible and how it corresponds to our subconscious minds. The Hebrew word translated heart is *leb*, which means "the feelings, the will, and even the intellect" or the "inner man."[24] Just before sending the deluge that destroyed all of humanity except Noah and his family, the Creator said of man that "every inclination of the thoughts of his heart was only evil."

He was making a statement about what was stored in man's subconscious mind—there was only evil there.

In the book of Proverbs, we read, "Let love and faithfulness never leave you; bind them around your neck, write them on the tablet of your heart." What is this "tablet" of the heart? The word refers to a polished board or plank that could be carved on and then read. What we "write" on our hearts we use as a reference for our attitudes and actions. Again, in Proverbs, we read, "To man belong the plans of the heart." The heart is where we sift things over and make decisions about what we want to do and be.

ALL OUR ACTIONS ARE MOTIVATED BY THE CONTENT OF OUR HEARTS.

The ancient book of Jeremiah the prophet records, "I the LORD search the heart and examine the mind, to reward a man according to his conduct, according to what his deeds deserve." The Creator examines the seat of our attitudes and sees what is stored there. He does this to reward a person according to what? His conduct or behavior. Attitude and behavior are tied together because your actions come from what you think. The writer of the biblical book to the first-century Hebrews said, "The word of God is living and active. Sharper than any double-edged sword, it penetrates even to dividing soul and spirit, joints and marrow; it judges the thoughts and attitudes of the heart." We are held accountable not only for our actions but also for our thoughts and attitudes. In the first book of the prophet Samuel, God said, "Man looks at the outward appearance, but the LORD looks at [studies what is in] the heart." This is because the subconscious mind reveals what a person really is.

Mark, the first-century writer and disciple of Jesus, recorded Jesus's words as he addressed the principle of focus: "Where your treasure is, there your heart will be also." Here is the principle: Whatever you value will preoccupy your mind, thoughts, and conscience. For instance, if you value earthly wealth more than the higher ideals of spiritual purity, goodness, kindness, faithfulness, and other noble attributes, then this will be your source of motivation.

Jesus also told a parable about forgiveness, concluding with the thought that "you [should] forgive your brother from your heart." Think about what this means when you consider that "heart" refers to the subconscious mind. You can tell someone that you forgive him, but in your mind, you can walk off and say, "I don't forgive you." Jesus is saying, in effect, "When you've freed the person in your subconscious mind, then you've truly forgiven him." You're not just giving lip service to it, but you've forgiven him in the depths of your being.

Again, quoting the words of Moses, Jesus said, "Love the Lord your God with all your heart and with all your soul and with all your mind." Both the heart and the mind are mentioned here. We are meant to love God with all our conscious and subconscious thoughts and attitudes. In essence, we are to have our conscious and subconscious minds filled with the thoughts, words, nature, attributes, and characteristics of God. The Creator should be the "default mode" on our mental hard drives.

Emphasizing the power of belief, Jesus told his disciples, "I tell you the truth, if anyone says to this mountain, 'Go, throw yourself into the sea,' and does not doubt in his heart but believes that what he says will happen, it will be done for him." You can mentally acknowledge something, but not doubting in your subconscious mind is a hard thing. That's why mountains don't move in our lives. Mentally or consciously, we say, "Go." However, the matter isn't truly settled within us. Our belief has to go deeper.

YOU DON'T REALLY BELIEVE SOMETHING UNTIL IT GETS INTO YOUR SUBCONSCIOUS MIND.

The beliefs and convictions of a leader regulate the nature of his leadership. You don't really believe something until it gets into your subconscious mind. Most of us can't break certain habits because we don't have the right thoughts and attitudes that will enable us to change. Your convictions determine what is stored in your heart, and your heart is the container of your attitudes. It's the bank you draw from that determines the way you live your life.

IDENTIFYING THE HEART

Your heart is the chamber that holds your convictions about all aspects of life. Your convictions are your beliefs, and your beliefs generally originate from what you keep hearing and believe to be truth. The heart is where all of what you have learned and repeatedly heard during your life is stored. It is also where all of your culture is assimilated into your psyche. It's the vantage point from which you view the world. Your heart is the seat of your beliefs. It is the center of your philosophy, the container of the ideas that you have accepted as truth.

Because, for the most part, the heart stores what you truly believe, and your attitudes and actions are based on those beliefs, the heart or the subconscious mind is the most dangerous component in your relationship to life. This is the reason why what you believe is essential—vital, critical—to your life. Your beliefs better be right because you live out of your heart; you see through your heart; you interpret through your heart; you judge through your heart. Developing the spirit of leadership means correcting what you have heard because much of what you have previously heard and accepted as truth has negatively influenced your image of yourself, your beliefs about your worth, and how you have lived your life.

YOUR HEART IS THE CHAMBER THAT HOLDS YOUR CONVICTIONS ABOUT ALL ASPECTS OF LIFE.

Why do you believe what you believe about yourself? As I mentioned earlier, the heart or subconscious mind is like a computer hard drive. It is the drive on which you have downloaded the software of your experiences and the information that you have received and accepted, as well as your evaluation of them. It stores all your ideas, beliefs, convictions, philosophy, experiences, memories, regrets, hurts, and secret thoughts. Whatever you put on your hard drive is what comes out when you press the right buttons.

To put it another way, you take out what you put in. If you want a chicken dinner, you can't put a snake into the pot and expect to get poultry. You have to put in the right ingredient. If we want to exhibit the spirit of leadership, therefore, it's important for us to receive the right information about what it means to be a leader. When we discover the truth, and that truth is established in our subconscious minds, transformation will occur. This principle is the reason people are able to have what is called a "change of heart." They change their attitudes and beliefs, and this alters their actions and reactions.

That's why it's important for you to get the right information. If you discover the truth, then the truth will make you free. If you do not erase, delete, or replace the information on the hard drive of your heart, then your leadership will be ruled, distorted, and influenced by whatever is in your default system. True leadership demands a constant monitoring of what goes into the heart.

YOU TAKE OUT WHAT YOU PUT IN.

The ancient Hebrew text of the Bible records wise King Solomon speaking of the power and function of the heart in his book of Proverbs: "Above all else, guard your heart, for it is the wellspring of life." Again, he is not speaking about the physical organ of the chest but rather the seat of all subconscious storage. Solomon's statement is an ancient saying, but the gravity of its meaning and implications makes it very difficult to comprehend. This statement teaches the reality that all our experiences and interpretations of life are not caused by external stimuli but rather by our internal state of being and beliefs. King Solomon also said concerning the power of the heart or subconscious mind, "As water reflects a face, so a man's heart reflects the man." The heart is the seat of life and determines the quality of our experience in life. **Leaders lead out of their hearts.**

In order to become the leader that you were created to be, you must pay attention to your heart, study what's in it, and consider the source(s) from which you received its content. You might be suffering from "hardening of the heart." Don't have a heart attack, but I challenge you to "attack" your heart and change its content to line up with the truth about you from the only sure Source—the Creator himself. Let his Word be the source of your words, then discover and believe the truth about yourself.

ATTITUDE AND ALTITUDE OF THE HEART

Ultimately, your subconscious *attitude* affects your *altitude*: The height to which your heart aspires depends on the information that is in it. You will know when you have captured the spirit of leadership because you will begin to see everything differently, and your new perspective will become the basis of your belief system. Rather than the environment influencing you, you will begin to influence your environment, starting with your mind-set.

Earlier, I quoted King Solomon, who said that "as a man thinks in his heart, so is he." Again, the word *"heart"* refers to the person's seat of reasoning, his subconscious mind, the center of his storage of learning. Solomon was saying that whatever you store in your heart determines how high or low you think about yourself and what you believe you can be and accomplish.

THE SOURCE OF THE SPIRIT OF LEADERSHIP

As we have seen, since our thoughts and beliefs generally come from what we internalize from our environments, we will become what we learn, listen to, and take in. We were originally designed to live in an environment conducive to the nature of God, which is the leadership nature, so that the source of our attitudes would be in-line with our purpose.

LEADERS LEAD OUT OF THEIR HEARTS.

You are what you believe. Your thoughts create your beliefs. Your beliefs create your convictions, your convictions create your attitude, your attitude controls your perception, and your perception dictates your behavior. What you truly believe about yourself creates your world. Remember that no one can live beyond the limits of his or her beliefs. In other words, your life is what you *think* it should be.

THE VITAL NEED FOR THE TRUTH AND FREEDOM

What all this comes down to is that the most important pursuit in life is the pursuit of truth. The ultimate leader of leaders, Jesus Christ, said that the truth will make us free. Free from what? Obviously, if I tell you the truth, you are free from an error or false information. He was therefore implying that whatever we learned before we received his information must be viewed with suspicion and, if necessary, deleted from our belief systems.

I mentioned earlier that, often, a person can have a title but not exhibit effective and true leadership. This is not because there is a problem with his title or because he isn't making enough money but because he doesn't know the truth about himself as a leader. A person can learn the methods and techniques of management and go through many leadership courses, but if he doesn't get this discovery of the truth, then his attitude will be defective. If his attitude is defective, his concept of himself will also be defective.

The first-century writer Paul, in his letter to the church at Rome, said that human beings did not retain the knowledge of God in their minds, and that is why they were corrupt. Somewhere along the line, the original software program files of humanity became corrupted, and now the program won't run correctly; it continues to spit out the corrupted information it took in. To use another analogy, if a pond's source of fresh water is cut off, it will soon become stagnant.

IF THE SOURCE OF YOUR THOUGHTS IS NOT CORRECT, YOUR THOUGHTS ARE INCORRECT.

If the source of your thoughts is not correct, then your thoughts are incorrect and your conclusions and beliefs are defective and contaminated—or will be soon. The result is a life lived in error and insecurity.

Therefore, discovering the truth is our most important pursuit, and the truth about us is found only in the Manufacturer. The famous question of history has always been "What is truth?" The most practical definition of truth I have discovered is "original information." A careful consideration of this definition reveals that the only one who knows the truth about anything is the one who created it, for only the originator would have original information about his product.

Consequently, any other statement about the product must be seen as only commentary or opinion. To rediscover the leadership spirit, we must go back to the Originator. To recapture the spirit of leadership, we must rediscover the truth—the original information—about ourselves from the Manufacturer.

In effect, the leadership spirit is the hardware and the spirit of leadership is the software. Developing the spirit of leadership means getting the original information for which our hardware was intended to work and operate. Again, the only one who has the original information of the product is the One who made it.

THE LEADERSHIP SPIRIT IS THE HARDWARE AND THE SPIRIT OF LEADERSHIP IS THE SOFTWARE.

It is interesting to note that the Hebrew concept of knowledge is "light," which implies that ignorance is "darkness." Revelation is therefore considered the light of the knowledge that God the Manufacturer possesses. As a matter of fact, God the Creator himself is described in the Bible as "light...[in whom] there is no darkness." The adversary of God and man is commonly referred to as the "Prince of Darkness." His power to control or rule a human spirit is generated by our ignorance. Man without the original knowledge of himself from the Manufacturer is like a lamp or a candle without a flame.

The book of Proverbs tells us that "the spirit of a man is the lamp of the LORD, searching all the inner depths of his heart." What happens when the light of that candle goes out? It needs to be relit. It needs original knowledge. Until God gives a human being the original knowledge of who he is, then he is a candle without a flame. He exists, but he has no real life. He doesn't have illumination about the way he has been designed.

It says in the Psalms, "For You will light my lamp; the LORD my God will enlighten my darkness." In other words, God will give the original knowledge, the information, that we need, enlightening us and removing our ignorance. Jesus said, "No one lights a lamp and puts it in a place where it will be hidden, or under a bowl. Instead he puts it on its stand, so that those who come in may see the light." First the Creator enlightens us, and then we are to go out and influence others with the light that he has given us. **True leadership is manifested when one individual uses his or her flame to light the lives of many and help them discover the reservoir of hidden oil in their own lamps.**

CHAPTER PRINCIPLES

1. True leadership is not a method, a technique, or a science but an attitude.

2. Having the spirit of leadership means that you understand and demonstrate the mind-set of a leader.

3. You have to choose to fulfill your leadership nature.

4. Manifesting the spirit of leadership is a matter of discovering and nurturing your true self so that you naturally evidence your leadership nature.

5. You cannot rise above the plane of your mental conditioning. To change your life, you must change your mind.

6. There is nothing more important than the *source* of our thoughts.

7. When your philosophy, beliefs, thoughts, and convictions are based on the way you were created to think, you will naturally rule over your environment and fulfill your life's purpose.

8. Our attitude toward life is largely a result of our self-concept or the picture we have of ourselves.

9. We are meant to see ourselves as being made in the image and likeness of our Creator and as having his nature.

10. Our thoughts and feelings about ourselves are determined by our self-worth. Since the Creator made us in his image and likeness, our value is a reflection of his value.

11. We can't lead if we depend on others to give us value, but only if we recognize our own inherent worth and what we have been given to offer others.

12. True leadership gives people a cause, a reason for living, and a sense of significance that gives meaning to their lives so that they feel necessary and purposeful. It gives them an outlet for expressing their own gifting.

13. In order to manifest the spirit of leadership, we have to acknowledge how our attitudes toward ourselves impact our relationships with others.

14. Self-esteem is your estimation of your value to the world. It is how you regard yourself in terms of your contribution and usefulness to others.

15. True leaders believe that they are needed by their generation and the world.

16. The greatest discovery in human experience is self-discovery.

17. Your leadership attitude—or spirit of leadership—will come alive when you discover and start living according to your true nature.

18. The best way to discover yourself is to discover God. When a person gets to know his Creator, and finally comes to know himself, then his leadership is born.

19. You don't really believe something until it gets into your heart or subconscious mind.

20. The most important pursuit in life is the pursuit of truth.

21. What you believe is essential to your life because you live out of your heart; you see through your heart; you interpret through your heart; you judge through your heart.

22. Developing the spirit of leadership means correcting what you have heard because much of what you have previously

heard and accepted as truth has negatively influenced your image of yourself, your beliefs about your worth, and how you have lived your life.

23. Your subconscious *attitude* affects your *altitude*: The height to which your heart aspires depends on the information that is in it.

24. No one can live beyond the limits of his beliefs. Your life is what you *think* it should be.

25. The beliefs and convictions of a leader regulate the nature of his leadership.

CHAPTER FIVE

THE LOSS OF THE
LEADERSHIP SPIRIT

The source is the authority and sustainer of the product.

I n our story from chapter one, something happened to cause the young lion to be separated from his fellow lions so that he was no longer in touch with his true self and believed that he was a sheep. Perhaps he was abandoned or left behind and then found by the farmer. In one way or another, he lost connection with the forest and found himself in an unnatural environment. Eventually, he came to accept his new surroundings as normal.

Likewise, we are living in an unnatural state. We have lost connection with our true selves and no longer have the mind-set that goes with our inherent leadership nature. How did this disconnect occur?

THE VITAL CONNECTION BETWEEN
SOURCE AND PRODUCT

In chapter three, I talked about one of the most important principles established by the creative process of the Creator: the principle of source and resource. This principle states,

A thing consists of the same material from which it came and must remain attached to its source in order to live and maximize its potential.

A brief review of creation and nature will reveal the truth of this principle for all living things. Everything the Creator made needs to remain connected to where it came from in order to fulfill its original purpose. For example, in the first book by Moses, we read, "And out of the ground made the LORD God to grow every tree that is pleasant to the sight, and good for food." The Creator made the trees from the soil, and they have to be connected to the soil or else they will die. Through the ground, their roots have access to the minerals and water that they need to stay alive. Similarly, a seed that isn't planted can never fulfill its inherent potential. It needs to become attached to its source in order to produce life. When a plant dies, it doesn't exist any longer in a form in which it can fulfill its purpose. It decays and turns back into soil—its original source.

Let's look at a related example: The Creator said, "Let the waters bring forth abundantly the moving creature that hath life." Fish and other sea creatures were created out of the waters, and that is why they need to stay in water in order to live.

The principle of source and resource also holds true for man-made processes such as manufacturing, which provides many of the products we enjoy. For example, if you want genuine parts for your car, you have to go back to the source that created the car. You don't go to another company; you have to get them from the authorized dealer. If you want to maintain a Rolex watch, you go to the Rolex company, not Timex. Likewise, if you want to repair a straw basket, you use the original material—straw—rather than stones.

THE SOURCE OF THE HUMAN SPIRIT

The most important application of this principle, however, is in relation to the creation of mankind. Let's consider again the origin of human beings to discover the nature of our connection with our Source. If you take a close look at the creation narrative, you will note that the Creator spoke to the material from which he desired the product to be made or created, and then out of the source material came the product.

A THING CONSISTS OF THE SAME MATERIAL FROM WHICH IT CAME.

As I noted earlier, when the Creator wanted vegetation, he spoke to the soil, and thus all vegetation originated from the soil, consists of elements in the soil, and must remain attached to the soil in order to live and be fruitful. The same principle is true of all living creatures. They all originated from the soil, consist of elements in the soil, and must be maintained by the soil. They, also, return to their source when they die.

However, when the Creator made the human species, remember that he did something unique and special: He did not speak to the soil, the water, or the atmosphere, but he spoke to himself. This fact is most critical for understanding the nature, composition, value, and worth of the human spirit. In fact, to produce the human being, the Creator actually used two processes. First, he said, "Let us make man in our image, in our likeness." When he made man, he essentially drew man out of himself, so that the essence of man would be just like him. Just as God is Spirit, he made humans to be spirits. Spirits, by nature, have no gender.

It is important to note that, in the Scriptures, there is no reference to a male or female spirit. This is because man, as an entity, does not *have* a spirit but rather *is* a spirit. The being that the Creator made in his image is much more than a physical being.

Next, we read, "God created man in his own image, in the image of God he created him; male and female he created them." The Bible also says, "The LORD God formed the man" and "made [the] woman." The Creator essentially took this spirit-man and placed him in two physical forms: male and female. The essence of both male and female is the resident spirit within them, called "man."

We can think of the distinction in this way: God *created* man, but he *made* male and female. The word for *"created"* is *bara*, and it means to form out of nothing.[25] The words *"formed"* and *"made"* are the Hebrew words *asah* and *banah*, and they mean to mold and build[26]—in this context, to mold and build out of something that is already there. In reference to how humanity came into

THE SPIRIT OF LEADERSHIP

existence, these verses say that God created man in his own image but that he also made man.

MAN, AS AN ENTITY, DOES NOT HAVE A SPIRIT BUT IS A SPIRIT.

Man was not created from matter; man came out of the Spirit of the Creator. The part of man that was made from "nothing" came out of God. The Creator just spoke him into existence, similar to the way in which He spoke, "'Let there be light,' and there was light." Yet when God made male and female, He used material from the physical world that He had already created. Humanity was given physical bodies in order to live and function in a physical world and to rule over it.

The original source of the spirit-man is the Creator, while the original source of our physical bodies is the dust of the earth. This is why our bodies eventually turn to dust when they die, while our spirits return to the Father of our spirits.

THE AUTHORITY OF SOURCE

As noted before, source is vital to the ongoing well-being of the offspring or product because it is the authority and sustainer of what it produces. The source from which something comes provides and determines its identity, ability, capacity, potential, and durability. The product is always linked to the source. For instance, suppose you have a wooden table, and I ask you what it is. You would probably respond, "It is a table." We label it *table*, yet, in it's essence, it's really a tree.

THE LOSS OF THE LEADERSHIP SPIRIT

Calling something a name other than one that connects it to its source doesn't negate what it intrinsically is—but it may limit its potential and usefulness in some way. That's why labeling people can be such a harmful thing. Our labeling dictates and controls our attitudes toward and our treatment of others. What is even more potentially damaging is that the people to whom we speak may internalize our labels, and this will limit their belief in their intrinsic potential and value. In the case of the table, its identity comes from its source, the tree. No matter what you say about it, its essential nature is derived from where it came from, not what you call it. The same is true for human beings. No matter what we might say is the nature of humanity, its true nature is derived from the Creator.

The only way for a person to know his true nature, then, is to go back and reconnect to his Source and see what he is made of. The essence of a human being is the spirit, not the body, so he has to go back to the Spirit out of whom he was drawn. Returning to the table illustration, there is much that we don't know about the table if we don't know the particular tree that it came from, the age of the tree, or what forest it grew in. We can sit at it, but we can't really tell its strength or durability because it has been cut off from its source. It's only as strong as the original tree.

The same principle applies to humanity. The human spirit can never know its leadership nature—its purpose, ability, potential, power, or anything else—without knowing its true origin and maintaining a connection with its Source. According to the principle of source and resource, knowing God isn't an option. We *need* to know him for our maintenance and survival. Again, any time you detach something from its source, things go wrong—it either malfunctions or it dies—because source provides all the following things:

Identity

Purpose

Concept

Worth

Value

Protection

Maintenance

Preservation

Productivity

Meaning

Life

THE GREAT SEPARATION

Just as a plant dies when it is detached from its source—the soil—or a fish dies when it is detached from it source—the water—if and when a person separates himself from his source—the Spirit of God—then he, too, will naturally malfunction and die. If you're severed from your Source, you're disconnected from all the items listed above. This is what happened to the human race.

The so-called fall of mankind was the disconnection of man from his source of creation—God—and the results were devastating. Human beings lost their sense of identity, self-worth, and self-concept, as well as their sense of personal value and significance to themselves, their world, and

THE LOSS OF THE LEADERSHIP SPIRIT

the universe. Basically, man lost the knowledge of who he is, where he came from, what he is capable of, where he is going, and why he exists.

WE FUNCTION BELOW OUR POTENTIAL BECAUSE WE WERE CUT OFF FROM OUR ORIGINAL PURPOSE.

We were cut off from our original purpose; therefore, we function far below our true abilities and potential, we lack the knowledge and wisdom necessary for making good decisions, and we suffer as the victims of our limited human knowledge and perspectives:

- We don't know who we are because we don't know from whom we come.

- We don't know the meaning of life because we're cut off from our original purpose.

- We can't be fully productive because we don't know where our ability and strength come from.

- We lack knowledge and wisdom for making good choices because we believe whatever seems right to our limited perspectives.

- We become fearful, apathetic, or overly competitive because we're trying to survive in an increasingly unnatural environment.

- We latch onto substitutes for the true Source in an effort to find significance and peace.

How did this separation happen? For the protection of humanity, the Creator established natural laws that corresponded with humanity's nature and well-being. Instead of trusting that these parameters were established for its own good, humanity declared independence from its Source. Essentially, human beings thought that they could live apart from their Source and therefore cut themselves off from him. All the problems of humanity that we see today and have seen throughout our history stem from this act. When you declare independence, (1) you have to create your own identity, and (2) you become responsible for your own destiny. The problem is this: If you don't have the resources for living independently—that is, if you don't intrinsically have life in yourself—then your failure is inevitable.

As the first man, Adam represented all of humanity. When he declared independence from his Source, he detached not only himself, but also all his future offspring, from true identity, purpose, protection, maintenance, preservation, productivity, meaning, and life. This is why the Creator warned Adam ahead of time, saying, in effect, "The day that you rebel against me by disobeying my command, you will surely die."

The concept of death here is not referring to the physical termination of the body, for according to the biblical account of the great separation, Adam lived for hundreds of years after his act of rebellion. Rather, death refers to the severing of the relationship man had with his Creator-Source. It refers to the demise of man's identity, sense of self-image, and self-worth. God was speaking of the spiritual death that comes from being cut off from our Source. The ultimate evidence of this death is manifested in the decay of the physical houses in which we live, the culmination of which we call death.

THE NATURAL RESULT OF SEPARATION

Any time a human rebels against the laws established by the Creator, death is the natural result. To the Creator, death is not ultimately the absence of life (spirit) from the body. True death—spiritual death—is the spirit being detached from its Source of life. Ultimately, what connected humanity to the Creator was his Spirit in us. When man disobeyed the laws of God, that Spirit departed, making the detachment complete. The result was that we had no direct way of relating to, communicating with, or receiving from the Creator. We lost both the power of the Creator and the consciousness of the spirit of leadership he had given us.

WHAT CONNECTED HUMANITY TO THE CREATOR WAS HIS SPIRIT IN US.

Therefore, when Adam cut himself off from the Creator, he was in rebellion against his natural state. A religious term for rebellion is *sin*. There is no word in Hebrew called "sin." The word most often translated as sin in English versions of the Old Testament is *chatta'ah*, which means "an offense, and its penalty."[27] The offense is basically a rebellion against one's Source, and the natural and inevitable penalty of the offense is death, or separation.

If you cut yourself off from your Source, it is you who will suffer, malfunction, and die, not the Source. Moreover, just as the soil never kills a plant or the water never kills a fish when they are separated from their source, it is not the Creator who does the killing. He doesn't have to. Death is a result, not an imposition. God's statement, "You will surely die," is just the announcement of a result, not a threat. He didn't say, "The day you do this, I will kill you." He said, "You will surely die."

If you pull a plant out of the soil, you don't need to kill it. It will wither on its own. If you take a fish out of water, you don't need to kill it. It will suffocate and die. Likewise, if a man takes himself out of connection with God, you don't need to impose destruction on him. He dies spiritually, and it's only a matter of time before he dies physically.

The Creator brought life, not death, into the world. He doesn't impose death on anything in his creation. Death is a result of rebellion against the natural laws established by the Source. These laws are in alignment with the nature and character of the Source and are for the optimum well-being of his offspring. Life is in the Source. Whoever stays attached to the Source will have life, just as a plant or a fish stays alive in its source.

The spirit of leadership is a natural derivative of the leadership spirit; it is the state of mind or attitude that emanates from it. Yet if we are cut off from the Source of that leadership spirit—when his Spirit has departed from our lives—we are also cut off from the attitude and power that should flow from our leadership nature. We end up distorting our leadership instead of reflecting it in the light of our Source.

THE LOSS OF THE LEADERSHIP SPIRIT

The leadership spirit is the inherent nature of the created spirit of man, which was released from the Spirit of God with all its qualities, characteristics, and potential. The spirit of leadership is the attitude and mentality that position reflects. We must realize that when man separated himself from his Source, he did not lose the leadership spirit, but he lost the spirit of leadership. In the next chapter, we'll talk more about the impact of our disconnect with the spirit of leadership.

CHAPTER PRINCIPLES

1. The "principle of source and resource" is that a product must be connected to its source for proper functioning.

2. When the Creator made various aspects of creation, he used just one process. Yet, when he made humanity, he used two processes: he *created* man, but he *made* male and female.

3. The original Source of the spirit-man is the Spirit of the Creator, while the original source of our physical bodies is the ground.

4. The essence of both male and female is the resident spirit within them, called "man."

5. Source is vital to the ongoing well-being of the offspring or product because it is the authority and sustainer of what it produces.

6. The only way for a person to know his true nature is to go back and reconnect to his Source and see what he is made of.

7. For the protection of humanity, the Creator established natural laws that corresponded with humanity's nature and well-being. Yet instead of trusting that these parameters were established for its own good, humanity declared independence from its Source.

8. Any time you detach something from its source, things go wrong because source provides all the following things: identity, purpose, concept, worth, value, protection, maintenance, preservation, productivity, meaning, life.

9. When a human rebels against the laws established by the Creator, then death—the severing of the relationship man has with his Source—is the natural result.

10. When mankind was disconnected from his source of creation, the results were devastating. Human beings lost their sense of identity, self-worth, and self-concept, as well as their sense of personal value and significance to themselves, their world, and the universe. Basically, man lost the knowledge of who he is, where he came from, what he is capable of, where he is going, and why he exists.

11. If we are cut off from the Source of our leadership spirit—when his Spirit has departed from our lives—we are also cut off from the attitude and power that should flow from our leadership nature.

12. The human spirit can never know its leadership nature—its purpose, ability, potential, and power—without reconnecting with its Source.

CHAPTER SIX

LEADING WITHOUT LEADERSHIP

Your attitude is more powerful than your reputation.

I magine that you have been walking along an isolated road for two days with no food or water and the sun is blazing down on you. Suddenly, you notice a well in the distance. Even though you are tired, you run with anticipation because you know that your thirst will be quenched. When you reach the well, however, you see a rope dangling over the opening, but no bucket. Deep down inside the well is what you need to satisfy your thirst and sustain your life, but you have no access to it.

This is a picture of humanity cut off from its life-giving Source. The leadership spirit exists deep down inside the makeup of every person because we are made in the image of our Creator and have an inherent dominion spirit. Yet we can't fully manifest this gift in our lives because we don't have the resources to access it. We have lost the Spirit of the Creator, and we have lost our awareness of the leadership spirit as well as the mind-set that enables us to exercise it effectively. Humanity's lack of connection with the Spirit of the leadership spirit has led to a loss of true leadership in the world.

THE IMPACT OF THE DISCONNECTION

Let's look more closely at our dilemma through two related illustrations. First, water is potentially a source of power. When it is harnessed, it can be used to run machinery, such as in a water mill. For this to happen, however, (1) you have to have access to the water, and (2) you have to have the machinery in place. If you are unable to harness the water or you don't have the proper machinery set up, then the mill can't fulfill its purpose. It's the same with the spirit of leadership.

THE LEADERSHIP SPIRIT EXISTS DEEP DOWN INSIDE THE MAKEUP OF EVERY PERSON.

The loss of the spirit of leadership is also like buying a new computer that has all the hardware to enable you to run programs and carry out their functions but then not having any power source to run the computer. Suppose, then, that you discover a power source and plug it in. The computer is powered on and ready to go, but you still need software for it to be of practical use to you. You have the knowledge of what the computer has been designed to do, and all the components of the hardware are ready for use. The potential is there, the ability is there, everything the manufacturer put into it is there, but it's almost as if you don't own a computer because you can't do anything with it.

These two examples illustrate the two-pronged nature of our problem. First, even though our potential as leaders is still within us, we've lost our connection with our Source of purpose and power. Second, even if the connection were to be reinstated, unless we obtain the right "machinery" or "software"—that is, unless we discover how a leader is meant to think and operate (the spirit of leadership)—we still won't be able to fulfill our potential. Simply put, **the leadership spirit is the inherent hardware, and the spirit of leadership is the software necessary for the hardware to function.** I'll be talking about these two crucial concepts in the next few chapters.

THE GREAT LOSS

In the Bahamas where I live, we are located in an area called the "hurricane zone." From time to time, we are subjected to the uncontrollable force of nature as the phenomena of the elements conspire to remind us of our vulnerability. During the hurricane season of 2004, when the monster hurricanes named Gene and Francis followed each other on a path right across our archipelago, I remember how helpless I felt. My wife and I made all our preparations and then sat waiting for the long-announced arrival of the category 4 and 5 storms. During one of the storms, the winds bore down on us like a living monster and shook the battened-downed windows. Suddenly, the electricity went out, and we were left sitting in darkness.

I reached for the flashlight and surveyed the room. Then I took a walk through the darkened house and checked everything to make sure the shutters were holding. As I examined the rooms with the flashlight, I noticed the many items we had accumulated that had become so important to us, but that now were completely useless: the large-screen television, VCR, CD players, air conditioners, computers, printers, and other high-tech "toys" we had purchased.

I stood there in the dark for a moment and thought about all the power, potential, benefits, pleasure, and untapped functions trapped in each of these items that were completely useless and unbeneficial to me at that moment. They existed, but they could not contribute to my present situation and life. They were filled to capacity with possibility, but they could not deliver. Why? Because they were cut off from their source, their power supply.

MAN IS A POWERFUL CREATURE FULL OF DIVINE POTENTIAL WHO HAS BEEN CUT OFF FROM HIS POWER SUPPLY.

I then saw a true picture of mankind: a powerful creature full of divine potential, talents, gifts, abilities, untapped capacity, creativity, ingenuity, and productivity, who himself had been cut off from his power supply. Now, he walks the earth living far below his intended privilege and capacity, victimized by his ignorance of both his Source and himself.

The loss of our Source of purpose and power has led to a myriad of negative outcomes because of the confusion that inevitably resulted. The following questions have been asked by countless generations since Adam declared independence from his Source:

❑ Who am I?

❑ Where am I from?

❑ Why am I here?

❑   What am I capable of doing?

❑   Where am I going?

These five questions summarize the essence of the human struggle and are what I, over the years, have called the questions of the human heart. They control everything that each human being does and are the motivation for all human behavior. All our social, economic, spiritual, and relational activities spring from the pursuit of answers to these questions. Until they are answered satisfactorily, there can be no personal fulfillment, and life will have no meaning. These questions address the five most important discoveries in the human experience: identity, heritage, purpose, potential, and destiny. They are the heart of the leadership struggle, and when answered, they give birth to true leadership.

WHAT DID MAN LOSE?

During the hurricane, as I looked at the computer sitting on my desk, I noted that the plug was still in the wall socket and that the physical casing and all its parts were still present. I also knew with reasonable certainty that the hardware and software were still intact. Again, the only thing that was missing, which prevented its function and operation, was the electrical power flowing from the source. Everything the manufacturer had promised that the computer could do was not able to be fulfilled or experienced because there was no power.

Man was created to function attached to God; he could fulfill his true potential and maximize his full capacity only through this connection. The key to effective and successful living was the indwelling Spirit of God—called the Holy Spirit. The Holy Spirit, therefore, is the key to true leadership. The Spirit is the critical component in every human's existence because he is the only hope for our rediscovering our true identity, self-image, self-worth, significance, self-esteem, and destiny.

WITH THE LOSS OF THE SPIRIT OF GOD, WE LOST OUR LEADERSHIP AWARENESS.

Again, with the loss of the Spirit of God from our spirits, we automatically lost our leadership awareness. Each consecutive generation since the fall of man has wandered farther and farther away from its leadership power. There is no true leadership without a reconnection to our Source, and only the Holy Spirit can reconnect us. He gives us our consciousness of the leadership spirit and is also the Source of the spirit of leadership.

A ROYAL SLAVE

The story is told of a prince who was born into a great royal family. When the prince was five years old, his father the king took the boy with him on a journey to a far country. During the journey, their ship struck a reef, and the entire crew and passengers were thrown into the angry waves.

During the turmoil and rescue effort, the little prince was saved by a native from a nearby island. The king was unaware of the rescue, and the little prince was now separated from his royal family. He became a member of the village and grew up unaware of his royal heritage. He learned to think and live like the natives and accepted this lifestyle as his own. In his poverty and simple life, he was not aware that he was from a wealthy family of high status and was heir to the royal kingdom of his father. In effect, he became a slave to the culture, customs, and standards of the community in which he found himself. He was a royal prince living under impoverished conditions. He did not know who he was, where he was from, why he was born, what he was capable of, or his rightful claim to be king. He lived his life vastly below his inherent privileges, not knowing the answers to the crucial questions of his life: his identity, heritage, purpose, potential, and destiny.

Knowing the answers to these fundamental questions gives a human being meaning and purpose. Without the answers, life is nothing but an experiment. This results primarily because of man's disconnection from his Source and manifests itself in the loss of humanity's original self-concept or image, self-worth, self-esteem, and sense of significance.

As I said earlier, every activity of man is a result of his attempt to find the answers to these questions. It is the reason we engage in the great human experiment of trying to find a sense of identity through our relationship to the world around us. I think that this may be why mankind seems to have an insatiable desire to explore space. It's a passionate search for where we fit in the scheme of the universe. It's a manifestation of the deep human search for significance.

This is also why we study primates. We are seeking to discover our true origin by finding perfect connections to other beings with which we share the earth. Unfortunately, this search will never be satisfied. We cannot know who we are by relating to creation because creation is not our source—the Creator is.

IN HIS SEARCH FOR SIGNIFICANCE, MAN USES CREATION AS THE CONTEXT FOR HIS SEARCH.

It is interesting that, in his search for relevance and significance, man continues to use creation as the measure and context for his search. However, it is essential to understand that we can never discover our value or purpose by studying the creation but only by a relationship with the Creator. God created the earth and everything in it for mankind and then gave humanity dominion over it. Everything in creation, therefore, get its significance from God and from us, not the other way around.

Because we are unaware of our intrinsic leadership nature, however, the average person is easily influenced by anyone or anything that seems to be stronger than he is. For example, instead of our having dominion over the earth, the earth has become our dominator in certain ways. Some people allow themselves to become controlled by drugs that come from plants. Others are enslaved to money, which is in reality trees that have been converted to paper and made into currency. Still others are controlled by grapes that have become fermented. People's lives are being destroyed by what is essentially vegetation. These are signs that we've lost our leadership awareness and ability. Imagine, sophisticated man with his immeasurable potential and intricate design being controlled by leaves and grapes. This is a tragedy and demonstrates how far we have been removed from our initial assignment of having dominion over all things in the earth.

I want to reemphasize that we haven't lost our inherent leadership spirit. We have lost our *connection* with the Spirit of the Creator, through whom we have an awareness of our intrinsic value and our leadership spirit, as well as the power to put it into effect. Again, we can think of the Spirit of the Creator as our original "default" mode. If we lose our original mind-set, then we will believe whatever is put on our hard drive instead of the truth about who we really are. To use another analogy, the leadership spirit has been obscured by the smoke of our social and cultural context, and we have become victims of the hazy opinions of "experts" who actually know very little about our true selves.

We were not created to be enslaved to other people's opinions, to our own passions, or to nature (creation). Yet man has become just like the animals because he now lives by instinct rather than discernment. This is why humanity as a whole has never regained its leadership awareness. Certain people—we saw examples of them in chapter two—capture glimpses of its truths and principles and apply them for effective leadership, but the full spirit of leadership is still not a reality in most people's lives.

In essence, the royal prince is the leadership spirit trapped in the culture and customs of a world that hides and suppresses his true spirit of leadership. He is simply a royal slave who was designed to rule but has been trapped in subjugation—a leader trapped in a follower.

AN IGNORANT KING

Another result of the disconnect is that, while we were designed to rule, we have become ignorant kings. Not only do we not know who we are, where we came from, and what we are capable of, but we also don't know how to use the resources that the Creator has given us.

Our brains are made up of millions of cells, but we tap only a fraction of our intellectual potential. Our bodies are intricately designed, yet many of us use our physical power and creativity to tear down rather than build up. We use them for violence, abuse, corruption, crime, and many other destructive things. Why would an intelligent, awesome creature such as the human murder his brother or sister, abuse his spouse, or commit incest against his own child? These things would be unthinkable to humanity in its original state. Yet, because of the disconnect, they have become a reality.

ALTHOUGH WE WERE DESIGNED TO RULE,
WE HAVE BECOME IGNORANT KINGS.

Psalm 82 in the Old Testament gives an intriguing commentary on the human condition. In this psalm, the Creator is speaking, and he begins by questioning the assembly of "gods," referring to mankind's status as a being who, although not equal to God, has been created in God's own image and likeness:

God presides in the great assembly; he gives judgment among the "gods": "How long will you defend the unjust and show partiality to the wicked? Defend the cause of the weak and fatherless; maintain the rights of the poor and oppressed. Rescue the weak and needy; deliver them from the hand of the wicked. They know nothing, they understand nothing. They walk about in darkness; all the foundations of the earth are shaken. I said, 'You are "gods"; you are all sons of the Most High.' But you will die like mere men; you will fall like every other ruler." Rise up, O God, judge the earth, for all the nations are your inheritance.

The Creator asks, "How long will you defend the unjust and show partiality to the wicked? [You should] defend the cause of the weak and fatherless; maintain the rights of the poor and oppressed. Rescue the weak and needy."

The Creator then explains the cause of mankind's behavior: "They know nothing, they understand nothing. They walk about in darkness; all the foundations of the earth are shaken." Darkness refers to their ignorance of truth, which results in evil actions. Because of their lack of justice, the very foundations of the earth are being shaken out of place. He adds, "I said, 'You are "gods"; you are all sons of the Most High.' But you will die like mere men; you will fall like every other ruler."

Some scholars say that the term "mere men" refers to mere flesh and thus means living from base animal instinct. Dogs don't have complex cognitive abilities; they have instincts. The Creator is basically saying, "I didn't make you like that. You're not a mere animal. You are in the 'god-class': You are made in my image and likeness and posses my nature and characteristics, and are therefore meant to rule with justice."

Compare this perspective to much of human behavior, and you will see that mankind has degenerated to engaging in inhumane activities. Moreover, this description of what happens when humans are not in touch with their Source is a graphic illustration of our present-day leadership dilemma.

If you read the questions and statements in this psalm, you will recognize the parallel to today. "How long will you defend the unjust?" In other words, in your courts, the criminal gets off while the victim is humiliated. This is because you're not in touch with yourselves. You can't even see the wrongness of your way of doing things. You're so corrupt; you go after money rather than righteousness or justice.

"How long will you show partiality to the wicked?" You give tax breaks to the man who is greedy while you burden the poor man with more than he is able to pay. That's showing partiality.

"Defend the cause of the weak and the fatherless." You don't take care of the orphans. You fill your stomachs full of food but let children sleep under bridges.

"Maintain the rights of the poor and oppressed." You don't look after people; you oppress them. All these questions are a demand for effective, competent, compassionate leadership.

He says that all this is going on because of the people's ignorance of who they truly are: God's image. That is why I think the term "ignorant king" is very valid. It explains why the leadership in our nations is so weak and inept and, at times, brutal and heartless. It is because of our detachment from our Source. Our Creator says, "What are you doing? You are completely the opposite of what I intended."

Mankind has become a kingdom of ignorant kings living under the mentality of an inferiority complex. It is from this context that many of our leaders emerge and attempt to lead us to a "better future." We long for leaders who think like true leaders.

MENTAL ILLNESS

The greatest impact of the disconnect, however, is what I call "mental damage" or "mental illness." The essence of this idea is that we have become what we think we are. The most powerful thing that a human has on earth, in my view, is his thoughts. The mind itself only contains the thoughts, so the thoughts are more important than the mind. **It is your thinking that determines your life.**

WE LONG FOR LEADERS WHO THINK LIKE TRUE LEADERS.

It seems as if most of the human race is suffering from mental illness, and it is epidemic among the majority of our leaders today. It is probably difficult for you to consider that many of our CEOs, administrators, managers, religious leaders, educators, sports heroes, scientists, and lawmakers are suffering from a grave form of mental illness, but in light of what we were originally created to be, this is a reality.

Some of our motivational leaders are mentally damaged. Many of our news celebrities suffer from mental illness. Our state legislatures and assemblies, national congresses, houses of parliament, and supreme courts are incubators for the mentally ill.

I'm not referring to people in an insane asylum. When I use the term *mental illness*, I am not referring to the medical definition of being psychologically incapable of sound judgment in relation to what we call normal in our societies. In the context of our discussion, I am referring to the inherent mental defect in every human being that resulted from our detachment from our Creator-Source. I am referring to the confusion we all face with regard to discovering our identity, self-worth, self-image, self-esteem, and sense of destiny.

Men and women of every nation, race, culture, status, and socioeconomic context all seem to be doing everything imaginable to fulfill their deep internal desires to find purpose, significance, value, and worth. A study of our modern and postmodern societies will reveal that no matter how sophisticated we may believe we are, we are still haunted by a passion to know who we *really* are. Many have tried even destructive behaviors to make some sense of their lives.

- They have power without purpose.
- They have money without meaning.
- They have position without a passion for living.
- They have houses but not homes.

- They have children but are not nurturing their sons and daughters.
- They protect animals but kill unborn human beings.
- They pursue power at the expense of principles.
- They sacrifice integrity for temporary pleasure.

These ways of thinking and living manifest a strange form of mental illness, which we have come to accept as normal. I sometimes think that most people in insane asylums are actually saner than many of us because at least they generally believe their worlds. It's the people who, deep down, don't really believe in what they're doing, but are doing it anyway, who are much worse off.

THE PERSON IN THE INSANE ASYLUM MAY ACTUALLY BE SANER THAN MANY OF US.

Isn't it amazing that many of us go every day to jobs we hate, live with people with whom we have no relationship, complain about everything while changing nothing, keep doing the same things over and over again—but expect different results? We exaggerate our accomplishments, pretend to be more than we are, hide behind false images of ourselves, and believe our reputations more than our true characters. Are we sane?

The result of mental illness is self-hatred, self-denigration, self-deception (denying the truth about oneself, lying to oneself), fear (fear of failure, fear of success, fear of the unknown, a general suspicion of other people, a distrust of God), ignorance of personal identity, ignorance of personal ability, ignorance of personal purpose, ignorance of a sense of destiny, and a mentality of survival (we don't really live—we just make a living).

The only thing that mentally ill people are sure of is death. In everything else, they live in uncertainty. That's why they're so suspicious and distrusting of others. Yet this is the mind-set from which we cultivate our leaders. We need help. (By the way, the insane never admit to their insanity, so if you disagree with this analysis, then perhaps you qualify!)

King Solomon, the wisest king who ever lived, wrote this statement in Ecclesiastes, his book on effective living and the challenges of life:

> There is an evil I have seen under the sun, the sort of error that arises from a ruler: fools are put in many high positions, while the rich occupy the low ones. I have seen slaves on horseback, while princes go on foot like slaves....Woe to you, O land whose king was a servant and whose princes feast in the morning.

Here, the great leader Solomon warned us that the home, company, classroom, community, or nation that is under the leadership of someone who has a slave mentality is in great danger. His statement also implies that being in a leadership position, in itself, does not guarantee mental soundness. In essence, wearing a crown does not change your mind. **Nothing is more dangerous than power in the hands of one who suffers from a sense of mental** inferiority. **The formula for oppression is power without mental soundness.**

THE FORMULA FOR OPPRESSION IS POWER WITHOUT MENTAL SOUNDNESS.

Now, imagine such a person being in charge of your life! Since humanity as a whole is suffering from mental illness, the bottom line is that these *are* the people we elect as leaders. These are the people who rule over us—whether it's as a manager, a supervisor, a company CEO, a judge, the chief of a village, a teacher in the classroom, a professor at a college, or the president or prime minister of a nation. They're mentally damaged and yet in charge of tens, hundreds, thousands, or millions of people! This is what today's worldwide leadership crisis comes down to.

WE CAN BELIEVE ONLY WHAT WE KNOW

Again, the cause of our mental illness is our detachment from our Source. Because we are ignorant of who we are, why we are here, where we came from, what we are capable of doing, where we are we going, and what our destiny is, our confusion produces mental problems. The alarming thing is that our mental state is the source of our attitudes because our thoughts and beliefs generate these attitudes.

The danger with this situation is that all we know is what we've learned, but all we've learned is not all there is to know. If what we've learned is not true, we will still live by it because we *think* of it as truth. We live and regulate our lives based on what we believe, and we believe what we've heard.

Our beliefs then become our philosophy, and our philosophy controls and regulates our lives and leadership.

A society generally cannot produce a leader better than itself because that leader usually gets his or her beliefs from the society. Therefore, basically, we appoint people who are no wiser than we are to lead and guide us. Every society should constantly check the source of the information by which it is living.

A SOCIETY GENERALLY CANNOT PRODUCE A LEADER BETTER THAN ITSELF.

Where do our beliefs come from? The word *belief* in the Greek language is *pistis*.[28] *Pistis* is the word that we translate as "faith." Every human being has faith—all seven billion of us. Even the atheist has faith. He believes that there is no God, so he has faith in no God. The question is, where did our beliefs, or faith, come from? They came from something we heard, imagined, or were taught.

Our leadership today is a product of the thoughts of our leaders, and therefore the saying is true: "As a man thinks in his heart [subconscious mind], so is he." When you want to study leaders and their leadership, do not study their physical appearance or demeanor. Study their hearts. Find out where they got their thoughts and ideas.

Hitler was simply the manifestation of the philosophy in his heart. He was a product of various influences, such as the teachers he had; the books he read; his family, friends, and associates; and his attitudes about his life experiences. His thoughts became his beliefs, his beliefs became his philosophy, his philosophy became his life, and, unfortunately, he lived out his philosophy with a distorted leadership influence.

The first-century leader Paul said that faith, or belief, comes by hearing something. We need to be listening to the words of our Creator. Why? Our hearing needs to be tuned to our Source so that our beliefs are based on original information, or truth. Again, the only one who knows the truth about a product is the manufacturer. Everything else is an opinion, an idea, or a suggestion. If we want leadership that is truthful, then our leaders must derive their source of belief from truth. Original information is found only in the mind of the manufacturer who created it.

THE LIMITED LEADER

There are three types of limitations in life. First, there are limitations that are imposed by external forces. Second, there are limitations that are inherent in the purpose and design of a created entity. Yet, most important, there is limitation that is a result of ignorance and faulty belief. This is the worst type of limitation because it is self-maintained and preserved. It is determined by us and not by others. In essence, **what we do not know about ourselves is limiting us**.

We are leaders, but we are limited because we do not know the truth about ourselves due to our disconnection from our Source. When Jesus Christ, the ultimate leader, was on earth, he taught certain things to reconnect us to the truth. For example, he constantly encouraged his disciples to do things beyond what they thought they were capable of doing. He kept moving them beyond the limits of their thinking because their attitudes were limited by their thoughts.

Leaders are limited by the extent of their knowledge of the truth about themselves and the world. The only one who knows the truth about all those things is the One who created them. We are not fulfilling our leadership potential because we are suffering the mental damage that results from our ignorance of the truth about ourselves and about creation. We have distorted beliefs because we have not been reconnected to the truth about ourselves.

The answer: We must somehow be restored to our Source. Regaining the spirit of leadership is about rediscovering and capturing the hidden knowledge about yourself and how to appropriate that knowledge in your everyday life. You are a leader by nature, and by design, you must discover the mentality that will set that leader free.

CHAPTER PRINCIPLES

1. The two-pronged nature of humanity's dilemma is (1) even though our potential as leaders is still within us, we've lost our connection with our Source of purpose and power, and (2) even if the connection were to be reinstated, unless we could discover how a leader is meant to think and operate (the spirit of leadership), we still wouldn't be able to fulfill our potential.

2. The loss of our Source of purpose and power has led to a myriad of negative outcomes because of the confusion that inevitably resulted.

3. Knowing the answers to the questions "Who am I?" "Where am I from?" "Why am I here?" "What am I capable of doing?" and "Where am I going?" gives a human being meaning and purpose.

4. When we don't know the truth about ourselves, we are just experimenting with our lives.

5. When human beings try to find the meaning of life, they often seek to gain their identity through a relationship with the world around them. We can never discover our value or purpose by studying the creation but only by a *relationship* with the Creator.

6. One result of our disconnect with the Creator is that we don't know how to use the mental and physical resources that he has given us. We use them for destructive things, such as violence, abuse, manipulation, corruption, and crime.

7. The greatest impact of the disconnect is that we have become what we erroneously think we are.

8. The most powerful thing that a human has on earth is his thoughts. It is one's thinking that determines one's life.

9. Confused thinking about one's origin and purpose results in self-hatred, self-denigration, self-deception, fear, ignorance of personal identity, ignorance of personal ability, ignorance of personal purpose, ignorance of a sense of destiny, and a mentality of survival.

10. We believe what we've heard and accepted as truth. Our beliefs then become our philosophy, and our philosophy controls and regulates our lives and leadership.

11. Generally, a society cannot produce a leader that is better than itself because that leader usually gets his or her beliefs from the society.

12. Leaders are limited by the extent of their knowledge of the truth about themselves and the world.

13. The home, company, classroom, community, or nation that is under the leadership of a ruler who has a slave mentality is in great danger.

14. If you want to study leaders and their leadership, do not study their physical appearance or demeanor. Find out where they get their thoughts and ideas.

15. To restore the spirit of leadership, our hearing needs to be tuned to our Source so that our beliefs will be based on truth.

CHAPTER SEVEN
THE RESTORATION OF THE LEADERSHIP SPIRIT

The Creator's purposes for mankind are permanent.

In this work, I have presented my position that every human was created with leadership potential and rulership capacity, yet few will discover this latent power and fewer still will release or manifest it. The question is why. Why is leadership so difficult to develop and manifest in our generation?

The answer, I believe, is not a lack of raw material or potential but the absence of right information, training, and an environment conducive to producing the mentality, mind-set, and attitudes necessary for this leadership potential to be ignited. This is *the spirit of leadership*. **True leadership has more to do with mind-set than with methods and techniques.**

In the story that opened this discussion, the young lion who thought he was a sheep, and who lived like and with the sheep, came to a point of decision where he either had to become himself or forever live in a world that was not designed for him. The young lion, as you will recall, made his decision and turned his back on the security and safety of the farm. He followed the great beast into the forest and was restored to his destiny, his reality, and himself. This is the challenge of all humanity—restoration to self.

TRUE LEADERSHIP HAS MORE TO DO WITH MIND-SET THAN WITH METHODS.

Despite humanity's declaring independence from its Source and manifesting the tragic and harmful results of its rebellion, the Creator hasn't changed his mind about his original purposes for us. He is passionately committed to our being reconnected to him for two principal reasons: (1) We are made in his image, and he doesn't want his image to be distorted or disgraced in the world, and (2) his purposes are permanent; he always accomplishes what he originally sets out to do.

THE PERMANENCE OF PURPOSE

As we have read in the original text of the creation narrative, the purpose for man's creation was to have dominion over the earth as ruler over the environment. Man was created to be a leader and was designed with the ability to manifest his leadership nature. The past and future of mankind is leadership. Leadership is your destiny.

The Creator is committed to fulfilling his purposes for us, which he initiated when he first created us. In order for him to accomplish what he originally purposed for us, he first has to reconnect us to himself. His original intent for mankind is the motivation behind his plan of restoration and all his interactions with us.

THE CORPORATE LEADERSHIP MANDATE

In this book, our philosophy of leadership is based on the precept that every human was created to be a leader. Again, if this proposition is applied to the traditional concept of leadership, which defines leadership as the management, control, or mobilizing of people, then the obvious question is, "Who will be the followers?" However, our principle is derived from the mandate established by the Creator when he said, "Let them rule ["have dominion"]...over all the earth." There are a number of important implications of this mandate that must be considered when discussing the purpose and assignment of mankind. Let's review them now.

1. The word *dominion* means to rule, control, govern, master, and lead.

2. The dominion command specifically referred to dominion over nature, not human beings.

3. The mandate to dominate, rule, and lead was given to the entire human species ("Let *them* rule") and therefore places every human in the position of leadership.

The implications of these truths are tremendous and critical. Each one a leader? How can this be? It becomes clearer when we truly come to understand that the mandate was for mankind to dominate fish, birds, plants, animals, and the entire environment of earth, but not his fellow-man.

This amazing mandate was the result of the Creator's purpose for mankind to be the reflection of a corporate leadership—in other words, a nation of kings, a company of rulers. The question then arises, "How does this type of leadership work?" The answer is in the concept of the servant leadership principle.

Each human being comes to earth with a specific gift, talent, and strength of ability. Each is to serve that gift to the others through subduing the material resources of creation and thus becoming a servant to everyone else. He or she becomes a leader in that specific area of strength.

God is described as King of kings, not king of slaves.

As we saw earlier, this principle of servant leadership was expressed by the ultimate leader, Jesus Christ, when he was asked about leadership positioning. Thus, the Creator's design of a corporate leadership can be summed up in the phrase "Every person a leader." Every human being, according to the Creator's mandate, was designed by him to be a leader in an area of gifting.

We must understand this truth if we're to fulfill the Creator's purpose: The command to have dominion over the earth was given to all of humanity. It wasn't given to a few select people, and it wasn't given to males alone. Both males and females are leaders, according to our Creator. God is described as King of kings. He is not the king of slaves but of rulers who reign with him according to his purposes. His plan for humanity is that each one be a king—a ruler over an area of gifting in creation.

Clifford Pinchot, a speaker and consultant on innovation management, is the author of the best-selling book *Intrapreneuring: Why You Don't Have to Leave the Corporation to Become an Entrepreneur.* He is also a contributing author in *The Leader of the Future*, published by the Drucker Foundation. Pinchot addressed the concept of corporate leadership in his work entitled *Creating Organizations with Many Leaders*: "Effective leaders today use the tools of community building to create an environment in which many leaders can emerge. They contribute inspiring descriptions of a shared vision to align everyone's energies....The organization of the future will be a community of entrepreneurs."[29]

As I read the many ideas being explored and introduced by leadership experts and gurus today, I am amazed that some of their so-called new ideas are simply old ideas that, for thousands of years, have been embedded in the texts of the ancient writings of the Scriptures. The Creator always intended that all men—male and female—become leaders in their specific areas of gifting and serve the world as a nation of rulers. Perhaps this is the notion behind the designation of Jesus Christ in his consummate relationship with mankind as the "King of kings." He is the Ruler of rulers, the Leader of leaders. This is the essence of corporate leadership.

THE PROGRAM FOR REPAIR—
RECONNECTION TO SOURCE

When humanity lost the spirit of leadership, the result was spiritual, mental, and physical decline. Human beings were disconnected from the Spirit of God, who enabled them to know the thoughts of their Creator. They had no other place to get their thoughts from, so they got them from themselves and their environment. This is what man has been living on ever since—his own thoughts, the thoughts of his contemporaries, and the deceitfulness of his adversary. What a combination to build one's heart out of!

The Creator's program for repair is to reconnect mankind to himself. We will call this reconnection "redemptive restoration." In its essence, the entire story of the Bible is about the Manufacturer refitting his product to accomplish his original purpose.

The Creator's prognosis of our condition is actually very different from what we usually think it is. It was not so much a "religious" problem as it is a thought problem. Therefore, he sent the Word (his thoughts) to earth to correct and redirect our thinking. The first-century writer John wrote,

> In the beginning was the Word, and the Word was with God, and the Word was God. He was with God in the beginning. Through him all things were made; without him nothing was made that has been made. In him was life, and that life was the light of men. The light shines in the darkness, but the darkness has not understood it....The true light that gives light to every man was coming into the world.

The Greek word that is translated *"Word"* in this passage is *logos*, which means "The Divine Expression."[30] Jesus is God expressing himself and his purposes to us. The Creator sent us his thoughts. When someone is sick, and the doctor does a diagnosis, the result of the diagnosis dictates the medication he prescribes. Therefore, God's prescription of sending his expressed thought indicates what

THE SPIRIT OF LEADERSHIP

he considered to be the source and cause of humanity's problem: a defective thought problem.

In the final analysis, our thinking creates our lives. Jesus came to give us back the original thoughts that we lost when we rebelled against our Source. When our thoughts are corrected, our attitudes will be transformed because our original thinking will be restored. This will ignite our leadership spirit and enable us to fulfill our leadership potential.

OUR THINKING CREATES OUR LIVES.

This is why, for three-and-a-half years, Jesus sat with his student-disciples—which included those businessmen who owned a fishing company, Peter, Andrew, James, and John—and challenged them to change their thinking by showing them the way a true leader thinks.

THE AUTHORIZED DEALER—JESUS

A few years ago, I purchased a new laptop computer and was intrigued when I read through the operator's manual. All the usual information was there, but what caught my eye were the last few pages at the back of the booklet. These pages dealt with the warranty and guarantee issues and the stipulation concerning using only an authorized dealer. The principle was clear: The company honored only the work of an authorized dealer in regard to repairs, and any violation of this agreement would cancel the warranty.

When a manufacturer addresses the issue of repairing a problem with its product, it has its authorized dealers take care of the situation because they represent the manufacturer and are familiar with the product. The same principle holds true in the case of the fall of man from his relationship with his Creator. The Creator sent his one-and-only Authorized Dealer to give us the original information about ourselves and to repair our damaged relationship with the Manufacturer.

The coming of Jesus to the earth was not so much a religious activity as it was a "business" transaction. His "assignment" was to do everything necessary to reconnect mankind back to his Source. Following our earlier analogy, Jesus came to restore power to the "computer"—he restored the Spirit of the Creator to our lives and gave us a new awareness of our purpose. Now we have the power to become what we were created to be. He restored our "hard drives."

JESUS'S COMING TO EARTH WAS MORE A BUSINESS TRANSACTION THAN A RELIGIOUS ACTIVITY.

We read earlier that "the Word is God." God sent himself to give us the true information about ourselves. Jesus said, "You will know the truth [through the Word], and the truth will set you free." Through the Word, we are set free from all the misconceptions and mental illnesses that resulted from our disconnection.

One of the statements Jesus made numerous times before he explained something was, "I tell you the truth." If you want to know the truth about yourself and the attitude you should have about yourself, you have to listen to the words Jesus spoke about you. We need truth, and he is the source of it. He said, "I am the way and the truth and the life." I read this as, "I am the way to the truth that gives you life." Put another way, he is the source of the information that makes us come alive.

John went on to say, "In him was life, and that life was the light [knowledge] of men." Jesus came to bring life. You never really live until you get true information about yourself. "The light shines in the darkness, but the darkness has not understood it." Darkness refers to ignorance, while light denotes knowledge. Jesus knows the truth about us—who we really are—and he is saying, "The more you know what I know about you, the more alive you will become."

"The true light that gives light to every man was coming into the world." Jesus knows the truth about every human being who is alive. That's why we go to him for restoration. It is not to "get religion," but to rediscover our Source and our true selves.

THE PROGRAM FOR REPROGRAMMING— THE RETURN OF THE SPIRIT OF THE CREATOR

The human spirit lost its connection with the Creator, which is the presence of his Spirit in our lives. Every act of the Authorized Dealer was a very intricate program that required certain things in order for the connection to be restored. First, humanity's rebellion had to be resolved because, remember, the rebellion resulted in a penalty: spiritual death. You can't cancel a penalty—someone has to pay it. Therefore, the Authorized Dealer took that penalty on himself. The substitutionary death of the Authorized Dealer was to satisfy the demands of the penalty for the rebellion of man.

The Restoration of the Leadership Spirit

This was the purpose of Christ's suffering and death. They were not ends in themselves but means for us to be fully reconnected and restored to the Creator. So now, this Spirit is available to every human being of every generation. The Authorized Dealer paid the penalty, provided complete forgiveness, and repaired the internal damage. We had been responsible for paying it, but we had no ability to do so. We never could have been restored without his intervention. After the repair, the Authorized Dealer's goal was to restore the Spirit to vessels who were now ready to receive him.

The last thing Jesus promised mankind was not heaven but power.

The last thing that Jesus Christ promised mankind was not heaven but power: "You will receive power when the Holy Spirit comes on you." He told his disciples, in effect, "I'm leaving to return to the Father God. My purpose on earth is completed, but I'm sending One who is just like me who will help you. I'm outside of you, and I'm demonstrating power, but he will be in you, and he's going to enact power through you and give power to you." Jesus knew that this power was what they were missing. It was what Adam lost. So the ultimate purpose of Christ's death and resurrection at Calvary was to return the power of the Creator to man so that he could fulfill God's intent for him.

The return of the Spirit of God to the spirit of man is the most important moment in human history since the Creator first breathed into man the breath of life and caused him to be a living being. We have the initial reception at creation, and then the re-reception at the end of the program of restoration. In this way, Jesus restored humanity's connection with its Source. At the same time, man's leadership spirit was reconnected to the Source of true leadership. The hard drive was restored, but now comes the more difficult part: the installation of the software of a renewed mind—in other words, the thinking of a leader.

THE NEED FOR A RENEWED MIND

Being a leader is a natural part of our makeup, but thinking like a leader is difficult. Although becoming reconnected is essential, it is just the start of developing into a true leader. We have to transform our thoughts and align them with those that our Creator is thinking. Paul wrote to the church at Rome, "Do not conform any longer to the pattern of this world, but be transformed by the renewing of your mind. Then you will be able to test and approve what God's will is—his good, pleasing and perfect will."

The only way to have a mind change is to rediscover the revelation of the truth about yourself—the reality that you were created and designed to be a leader. You must internalize the truth that leadership is your nature, your destiny, and your purpose for existence. You must capture the essence of the understanding that the purpose for your existence is to have dominion over the earth. You were born to rule—to lead. Once you capture this truth, then the work begins.

The mental transformation—in our computer analogy, this would be the downloading of new software—is different from the repair and restoration. It is a process that takes time because it involves the changing of ingrained thoughts and habits. The vital difference is that now you have the power and the access to the Spirit of the Creator that will enable you to be able to do this.

The return of the Spirit restores to us the consciousness of our leadership spirit and dominion assignment. Now comes the challenge, which is what the rest of this book deals with: the transformation of our minds as we discover and live out the attitudes of the spirit of leadership. The essence of this book is about the downloading of the leadership software.

CHAPTER PRINCIPLES

1. True leadership has more to do with mind-set than with methods and techniques.

2. The challenge of all humanity is restoration to self.

3. Despite humanity's declaring independence from its Source, the Creator hasn't changed his mind about his original purposes for us.

4. The Creator is passionately committed to our being reconnected to him because (1) we are made in his image, and he doesn't want his image to be distorted or disgraced in the world, and (2) his purposes are permanent; he always accomplishes what he originally sets out to do.

5. The Creator's ultimate purpose for humanity is to create a corporate leadership, summed up in the phrase, "Every person a leader." The command to have dominion over the earth was given to all of humanity, males and females.

6. Corporate leadership works through the servant leadership principle.

7. Every human being, according to the Creator's mandate, was designed by him to be a leader in an area of gifting.

8. The Creator's program for reconnecting humanity with himself can be called "redemptive restoration."

9. Humanity's dilemma is not so much a "religious" problem as it is a thought problem.

10. God sent "the Word," Jesus Christ, to earth to correct and redirect our thinking. He came to give us back the original thoughts that we lost when we disconnected from our Source.

11. When our thoughts are corrected, our attitudes can be transformed, and we will be able to fulfill our leadership potential.

12. The Authorized Dealer, Jesus, is "the way to the truth that gives us life."

13. You never really live until you get true information about yourself.

14. The substitutionary death of the Authorized Dealer was to satisfy the demands of the penalty for the rebellion of man. Through his death, humanity could be fully reconnected and restored to God, and the Spirit of the Creator was made available to people of every generation.

15. The ultimate purpose of the suffering and death of Jesus Christ was to return the power of the Creator to human beings so that we could fulfill God's original intent for us.

16. The return of the Spirit restores to us the consciousness of our leadership spirit and dominion assignment.

17. Full restoration of the spirit of leadership is a process of transforming our thoughts and aligning them with those of our Creator.

18. Mental transformation is different from repair and restoration. It is a process that takes time because it involves the changing of ingrained thoughts and habits.

19. Through the Spirit, we have the power and the access to the Creator that will enable us to effect a transformation of our attitudes.

CHAPTER EIGHT
LEADERSHIP ABILITY WITHOUT THE ATTITUDE

No leader can rise above his attitude.

When the young lion saw the older lion and reconnected to his true nature, the process of his growth was still ahead of him. He knew his identity, but he had to understand what that identity really meant. Only by entering the right environment—the forest—could he discover what it would involve for him to someday take his place as king of his domain. The same is true for us.

HARDWARE WITHOUT SOFTWARE

As I wrote in the previous chapter, when we are restored to our Source of power, we are still missing a key element: the software. The software is our leadership attitude. We have been detached from this attitude for so long that, even though we now have an awareness of our leadership spirit, we need to take on the mentality of a leader because we still have the mind-set of slaves.

THE MIND OF THE SPIRIT AND
THE SPIRIT OF THE MIND

The greatest challenge of those who have been reconnected with the Creator is having their attitude correspond with the mind of God's Spirit who now dwells within them. Jesus has provided for the restoration of the Spirit in us. We are spiritually reconnected to our Source, but the second step is that of restoring the attitude of our minds so that we can exercise our leadership spirit.

Paul said, "Your attitude should be the same as that of Christ Jesus," and "Be renewed in the spirit of your mind." He was talking to people who had already received God's Spirit, so he was indicating that they had not yet changed in the way they needed to. Just because we've been reconnected to our Source doesn't mean that we are thinking like him in all ways. Our attitude needs to be adjusted. Only when we are renewed in the "spirit of our mind" will we have the attitude that reflects the mind of the Spirit.

THE HEART AND THE MIND OF LEADERSHIP

Remember our earlier discussion about beliefs being our own only as they move into our subconscious minds? In your mind, you can know that you are a leader, but if this knowledge is not in your subconscious mind, then you still won't behave like a leader. If your heart is not changed, then you're a new creature with an old mind.

Jesus, the great leadership trainer, would often say, "He who has ears to hear, let him hear." Some people just want to listen; they don't want to hear, so it never gets into their subconscious minds. The only way to get things into your subconscious mind is through repetition. You have to "download" it over a period of time. When you download something onto your computer, you have to wait until it is finished before you can use it. You can't force it to download. It is the same with your heart. You have to patiently allow the new information to settle into your subconscious. For example, it may be necessary for you to read this book three or four times to absorb all the leadership information that it contains.

Salvation Is Different from Conversion

Salvation (reconnection with God) is not necessarily synonymous with conversion (the transformation of the mind). The word *conversion* in Greek means "reversion" or "a turning about."[31] Although salvation is a turning back to God, we also need to be coverted in the sense of reverting to the original information the Manufacturer gave us. It is through the Spirit of the Creator that we can mend the attitude of our minds because he is the Spirit of Truth who reminds us of the truth that the Authorized Dealer brought us.

You have the capacity to lead, but you need the mentality for it.

In other words, in leadership terms, salvation should not be confused with conversion. You will never become a true leader until you discover how to *think* like a leader. You have the capacity to lead, but you need the mentality for it. You have the ability to lead, but you need the understanding to do it. You have the potential to lead, but you need to have a revelation of leadership.

There has to be a conversion in your heart or subconscious mind that creates a different sense of reality for you. When you think in a different way, you will become different. Your head has to catch up with what has already happened in your spirit. What's been in your subconscious mind for the last ten, twenty, or thirty years is going to fight what the Spirit is revealing to you. Whether it was a parent who said you were no good, a teacher who told you that you weren't smart, or even a well-meaning pastor or priest who told you to be "humble," various people have negatively influenced your perspective toward your leadership ability.

How many times have you agreed with something yet did not do it? How many times have you said to yourself, "That's true," but did not act on it? You believed it because it was true, but you were not to the point of conviction where it caused you to act. You probably believe that there are certain things you cannot do, and you think things such as the following: "I don't deserve this." "I can't go there." "I can't achieve that." "There's no way I can have that." "I can't even *think* about that." You have to come to believe that you can pursue and accomplish what the Creator has already put within you to do.

LEADERSHIP—ATTITUDE OR APTITUDE?

Remember that leadership is both an aptitude and an attitude. No matter how much intellectual ability you have, if you don't have the right attitudes, your ability doesn't mean anything. Winston Churchill said, "Attitude is a little thing that makes a big difference."[32]

When I was in college, I signed up for a class in business administration. Then I discovered that the professor was driving a VW and wearing torn jeans and old shoes. He walked into the classroom and said, "Today our session is about how to become a millionaire." I sat there and said to myself, *I'm in the wrong class.* I dropped the course because he had an aptitude, but obviously he didn't have the attitude that would enable him to achieve what he was about to try to teach me. Something was missing.

WHEN YOU THINK IN A DIFFERENT WAY, YOU WILL BECOME DIFFERENT.

The wealthiest people in the world are usually not intellectuals or academic experts. I'm not saying that they aren't intelligent but that their financial success is not attributed to their educations. Computer entrepreneurs Bill Gates and Steven Jobs are examples of successful people who didn't do well under a traditional educational experience. Although they dropped out of college, they somehow had a certain attitude that caused them to be convinced that they had valuable ideas to develop. They discovered purpose and passion, they believed in their ideas, and they inspired other people who believed in them, too. Eventually, hundreds of thousands of people bought their products—and still do.

In chapter two, I gave examples of leaders who found a purpose and a passion and inspired others to follow them in their visions. Yet they were not overnight successes. They had to have the right attitudes and then persevere in them in order to be effective.

Abraham Lincoln is a classic example of this. He failed to accomplish his goals many times, but he had an inner belief that he had something to offer his community, his state, and eventually his nation. This attitude is what kept him in the race even when he faced negative circumstances and setbacks. How do you react when you fail? You have to have an inner belief that is stronger than your experience. Victor Frankl, the holocaust survivor, said, "It's not what happens to me that matters, but what happens in me."

Sir Winston Churchill is another good example of someone who persevered in his vision and in pursuing what he believed was right. He understood clearly that Nazism was a threat to Great Britain and the world, but he spent months and years as essentially the lone voice of warning before others realized the truth of what he was saying. He had an inner conviction that kept him going. Under the pressure of circumstances and a sense of responsibility for saving the nation of England, his leadership developed and matured.

In a sense, George W. Bush's presidency was born on September 11, 2001, when terrorists crashed planes into the World Trade Center buildings in New York City, the Pentagon in Washington, D.C., and a field in rural Pennsylvania. This crisis introduced Bush to himself. The demands and responsibilities of his position put tremendous pressure on him, and the result was a new attitude of deep responsibility for the welfare of the citizens of America that brought out his inherent leadership ability.

You might know that you are a leader. That's awareness. But do you have the mental conditioning to manifest that reality?

"We cannot choose how many years we will live, but we can choose how much life those years will have."
—John Maxwell[33]

CHAPTER PRINCIPLES

1. Leadership is both an aptitude and an attitude.

2. No leader can rise above his or her attitude.

3. Man's greatest challenge is having his attitude correspond with the mind of the Spirit of God within him.

4. The *mind of the Spirit* is the presence of the Spirit of God in man's spirit, but the *spirit of the mind* is the attitude that accompanies that Spirit.

5. Salvation (reconnection with God) is not necessarily synonymous with conversion (the transformation of the mind). The word *conversion* in Greek means "reversion" or "a turning about." We need to revert to the original information the Manufacturer gave us.

6. It is through the Spirit of the Creator that we can mend the attitude of our minds because he is the Spirit of Truth who reminds us of the truth that the Authorized Dealer brought us.

7. You have to patiently allow the new information from the Creator to settle into your subconscious.

CHAPTER NINE

RECAPTURING THE SPIRIT OF LEADERSHIP

The key to the spirit of leadership is attitude rather than aptitude.

A few years ago, my wife and I went to Egypt and had a tour of the pyramids. We saw the tombs of the Pharaohs, as well as a chariot and a gold bracelet owned by one of the Egyptian rulers. The artifacts were in glass cases. In one case, there were some seeds of corn, wheat, and maize. The notation said something like, "These seeds were found in the Egyptian desert, not far from the Nile, where it is so hot that anything that is underground can be petrified and preserved for thousands of years. These seeds are 6,000 years old."

The sign also said that some of the ancient seeds had been germinated. The Egyptian government had taken seeds that were 6,000 years old and planted them, and the seeds actually grew! When they crossbred the ancient seeds with modern seed, they found they got a better crop.

These seeds were underground for 6,000 years, but they never lost their innate potential. They were destined to become what they had been created to be: fully grown plants that could nourish people. No matter how long you have been "petrified" by your emotions, the circumstances of life, or others' opinions, your innate potential is still within you. The Authorized Dealer connects you with the Creator so that you can fulfill your destiny and do the work you were born to do. Paul wrote to the first-century church at Philippi, "We are God's workmanship, created in Christ Jesus to do good works, which God prepared in advance for us to do."

THE GOAL OF THE CREATOR IS TO RESTORE THE SPIRIT OF LEADERSHIP BACK TO THE MIND OF MAN.

The goal of the Creator is to restore the spirit of leadership back to the mind of man. To accomplish this, God sent us his Word. God's words are designed to transfer truth and ideas that will renew our thought lives and thus transform the spirit of our minds, our attitudes.

THE POWER OF MENTAL CONDITIONING

Our mental conditioning determines our success or failure. You have to train to become what you want to be. The reason soldiers are sent to boot camp is to get them to stop thinking like civilians and start thinking like professional military minds. In boot camp, they are isolated from their families and friends and the rest of society so that they can focus on their new mind-set.

Similarly, when you want to change your mental attitude about leadership, you have to train yourself. You will find that the power of mental conditioning will sustain you and give you the internal fortitude to overcome incredible odds. Our beliefs are housed in our hearts, but they manifest themselves as we experience various circumstances. The level of your mental conditioning dictates your response to life, to issues, to circumstances, to creation, to your world. This is why one of the most powerful things you possess on earth is your mental attitude. As you take in the thoughts of the Creator through prayer and reading the Bible, the Spirit "downloads" these truths to your heart so that your mind is trained to rely on his thoughts and not your former distorted ideas about life.

THE SPIRIT "DOWNLOADS" THE CREATOR'S THOUGHTS TO YOUR HEART.

Jesus said that the Spirit would teach us the truth and explain the things that he has said. He will be our teacher. In order to have the right mental attitude, you have to have the right teacher, and your teacher, according to the Creator, is his Spirit who dwells in you, who takes up residence in you for that very purpose. Leadership demands mental reconditioning.

THE MARRIAGE OF ABILITY AND ATTITUDE

When you practice renewing your mind, you begin to recapture the spirit of leadership. In this way, there is a marriage between who you inherently are as a leader and the way you are meant to think as a leader. **When the attitude of leadership is married to the ability of leadership, then you are a true leader.**

INTEGRATING LEADERSHIP MENTALITY AND THE LEADERSHIP MANDATE

The Creator has given us a mandate to lead and have dominion over an area of life. However, we have to integrate this responsibility with the necessary mentality. We can never fully carry out the mandate of leadership if we don't have the mentality of leadership.

INTEGRATING ATTITUDE, ATTRIBUTES, APTITUDE, AND ALTITUDE

Leaders think in a certain way. Therefore, they manifest certain attributes and they work hard to attain a certain aptitude (they continually desire to learn more about themselves, life, and God), and this causes them to think at a higher level, or altitude. The more truth about yourself that you receive into your heart, the higher your thinking will be. You will have an increasingly clear vision for your life. All these areas need to be integrated for effective leadership.

THE KEY TO THE SPIRIT OF LEADERSHIP: ATTITUDE

Again, the key to the spirit of leadership is attitude rather than aptitude. In other words, **it's not ability—it's mentality.** What you think is even more important than what you do. The chapters that follow explore essential attitudes that must be cultivated for you to experience and achieve your fullest leadership potential.

A leader has to have an integration of attitudes. You can't have vision without courage, you can't have courage without compassion, and you can't have compassion without strategy if you want to be an effective leader.

Attitude is a learned behavior, created by our beliefs, which are produced by our thoughts. We change our attitudes by changing our beliefs, by changing our thoughts about everything in life—including ourselves. Ralph Waldo Emerson said, "What lies behind us and what lies before us are tiny matters compared to what lies within us."[34] The first-century writer John said, "The one who is in you is greater than the one who is in the world."

ATTITUDES CAN BE CHANGED

We can change our attitudes. In fact, we are responsible for doing so. We cannot continue to function in a manner that we do not truly believe about ourselves. The day that we take responsibility for our attitudes is the day that we truly grow up.

Attitude determines everything. It is not enough to know the principles, precepts, and skills of leadership. We must acquire the spirit of leadership by discovering and applying the attitudes of true leaders. **Training in leadership really means training in attitude because attitude has to do with how we respond to life. We must think, talk, walk, dress, act, respond, decide, plan, work, relate, and live like leaders.**

I have had to learn the attitudes of leadership. I was born in a very poor neighborhood in the Bahamas, in a wooden house on four stones. I had ten brothers and sisters, and I slept on the wooden floor of our two-bedroom house. I grew up in a neighborhood where there was poverty, and questionable characters were always present, exerting a negative influence.

Then I went through a transformation. I desired to know the truth about my life and about life in general. I questioned my disposition and challenged the status quo during my teenage years. The answers began to appear when I was given a Bible by my parents at age thirteen. I discovered in the pages of this book the amazing truth that I was created in the image of the Creator and that his intent was for me to know him and his will for my existence.

WE ARE RESPONSIBLE FOR CHANGING OUR ATTITUDES.

This discovery changed everything for me forever. When I began to read the Bible, I received new thoughts about myself and my world. The source of our thoughts is so important because our thoughts are the key to our quality of life. When I read the Bible, it contradicted what I was taught and what I saw with my eyes. I began to believe what it said rather than what I heard from outside sources, and that is how I developed a leadership mentality.

Whatever your own circumstances, you, also, can experience the transformation of your outlook as you discover the attitudes that will enable you to be the leader that you were born to be.

CULTIVATING THE LEADERSHIP SPIRIT

In my experience, leadership is 20 percent talent, skill, and technical knowledge and 80 percent attitude. Most of the great leaders throughout history possessed a unique self-perception that set their characters apart from the average person. A careful study of these leadership giants will reveal that they weren't born with this attitude, but it was ignited in them and then cultivated by a life-changing encounter with the Creator.

To cultivate means to grow, progress, and cause the orderly development of something. This process demands that the right components, resources, and environment be incorporated into the soil of the system. **Cultivating the spirit of leadership is a choice, and only you can make it.**

The most outstanding leaders we can study are biblical characters, such as Abraham, Sarah, Moses, Joshua, Gideon, David, Daniel, Esther, Deborah, Jeremiah, Mary, Peter, Paul, and John. In every one of the above cases, you will see that they experienced personal encounters with the Creator of mankind and, in these encounters, were challenged to believe things about themselves that they found difficult or almost impossible.

The Creator challenged their views, images, and conceptions of themselves and made demands on their potential that they did not believe they possessed. Moses, a fugitive, was challenged to become a "union leader," a "freedom fighter," and a national political leader destined to build a nation that would change the world. Moses's fear of others, poor sense of self-worth, and low estimation of his own abilities were challenged by the Creator, and he was commanded to go and deliver the charge of "let my people go" to the most powerful government of his day. His self-concept, self-awareness, and estimation of his ability changed almost overnight, and the spirit of leadership was ignited within him. His attitude was changed forever.

Joshua, Moses's assistant, was challenged to take leadership responsibility for millions of desert people and to settle them in the land of promise, establishing social, cultural, and economic institutions for the new nation. His timidity was challenged by the Creator, and he was commanded to "be strong and courageous." His self-concept changed in that encounter. This new perception of himself produced the spirit of leadership in him and an attitude that distinguished him from other people.

The same scenario of transformation played out in the lives of Gideon, David, Esther, and all the others. Their personal encounters with their God challenged their self-images, self-concepts, self-esteem, self-worth, and sense of potential. It also gave each a sense of purpose for their lives and changed their attitudes forever. The spirit of leadership was ignited in each, and their lives impacted their generations and continue to inspire the world today.

CULTIVATING THE SPIRIT OF LEADERSHIP IS A CHOICE.

What is crucial in all these cases is the fact that all of them had images of themselves that were not correct and were produced by their cultures, past experiences, or the opinions of others. This is the reason the hidden leader within all of us remains buried and suffocates in the grave of our mediocre cultures. To be free from this condition, we must determine to cultivate the spirit of leadership and rise above the limitations of our past experiences, other people's opinions of us, and the stifling context of our so-called social norms.

As I noted earlier, to begin this process, we must ask ourselves some very important questions, such as "What image do I have of myself?" or "How do I see myself?" and "What do I imagine that I am capable of?" Self-image sets the boundaries of both individual and national accomplishment.

It defines what you can and cannot be or do. Expand the self-image, and you expand the scope of possibilities. As in the above examples, most of our self-images are the products of our primary role models, our historical context, our formal and informal educational training, and our social environments and powers of influence.

It is important to understand that the world usually forms its opinions of you primarily from the opinions you have of yourself. Others often see you in precisely the way you see yourself. You will generally act in a way that is consistent with your self-image. Self-esteem is the emotional component of your self-concept and represents the real core of your human personality. This is true of individuals and nations alike. It deals with the question, "How do you feel about yourself?" How much you like yourself is totally dependent on who you think you are. **How you define yourself is the single most important statement you can make about yourself, and it is the heart of attitude. The spirit of leadership will emerge from your self-definition.**

You act in a way that is consistent with your self-image.

Low self-esteem is a result of an inferiority or superiority complex. Again, the way you relate to others is directly connected to how you feel about yourself. This is why Jesus's response to the question, "Which is the greatest commandment in the Law [of God]?" was, in effect, "Love your neighbor as much as you love yourself." The value that you perceive others to have and the way you treat them is directly determined by how you see and value yourself. You can never truly value others above your own value.

All behavior is shaped and controlled by who and what you think you are. Everything in life is indeed attitudinal. Your self-image determines the level of your self-esteem and self-worth. Your self-esteem determines how you live your life. In the final analysis, **your ability to lead depends on the attitude produced by your self-image, sense of self-worth, and self-esteem.**

Marks of the Spirit of Leadership

Just like the many examples of effective leaders discussed earlier, when you rediscover the truth about yourself, then you, too, will ignite the process of developing the marks of a true spirit of leadership:

- the spirit of a strong self-image—a true sense of one's Source

- the spirit of a healthy self-concept—a perception of one's true nature

- the spirit of self-confidence—a belief in one's inherent ability

- the spirit of self-significance—a sense of valuable contribution to the world

- the spirit of passion—a deep conviction and determination of heart

- the spirit of excellence—a striving to always improve oneself and one's work

- the spirit of compassion—a sensitivity to the value of others

- the spirit of creativity—a belief in the untested and untried

- the spirit of self-empowerment—a desire to see others succeed

- the spirit of self-improvement—a personal commitment to grow

- the spirit of self-discipline—a commitment to a self-imposed standard

- the spirit of humility—a consciousness of self and one's strengths and weaknesses

- the spirit of unlimited ability—a belief in one's potential as raw material

- the spirit of possibilities—a commitment to unlimited thinking

- the spirit of self-acceptance—an embracing of one's total humanity, including one's strengths, weaknesses, personality, physical appearance, defects, and gifts

In the following pages, I want to address the heart of this book, and that is the qualities and characteristics of the spirit of leadership—the unique attitudes that all true leaders possess, and the fact that you can cultivate and develop them. These attitudes are necessary if you are to experience the manifestation of your leadership capacity. They can be learned, developed, cultivated, and refined through practice and responsibility. When they come together in your life, then you will fulfill the definition of a leader: You will have the capacity to influence others through inspiration motivated by a passion, generated by a vision, produced by a conviction, ignited by a purpose. To paraphrase Paul Meier,

*Attitudes are nothing more than habits of thought
produced by your self-image, self-worth, and
self-esteem, and habit can be acquired and changed
by the reconditioning of the mind.*[35]

CHAPTER PRINCIPLES

1. No matter how long you have been "petrified" by your emotions, the circumstances of life, or others' opinions, your innate leadership potential is still within you.

2. God's words are designed to transfer truth and ideas that will renew our thought lives and thus transform the spirit of our minds, our attitudes.

3. Our mental conditioning determines our success or failure.

4. When the attitude of leadership is married to the ability of leadership, then you are a true leader.

5. Leaders manifest certain attributes, and they work hard to attain a certain aptitude (they continually desire to learn more about themselves, life, and God), and this causes them to think at a higher level, or altitude.

6. The day that we take responsibility for our attitudes is the day that we truly grow up.

7. We must acquire the spirit of leadership by discovering and applying the attitudes of true leaders. We must think, talk, walk, dress, act, respond, decide, plan, work, relate, and live like leaders.

8. Leadership is 20 percent talent, skill, and technical knowledge and 80 percent attitude.

9. Cultivating the spirit of leadership is a choice, and only you can make it.

10. How you define yourself is the single most important statement you can make about yourself, and it is the heart of attitude. The spirit of leadership will emerge from your self-definition.

11. All the leadership attitudes can be learned, developed, cultivated, and refined through practice and responsibility.

12. When the leadership attitudes come together in your life, then you will fulfill the definition of a leader: You will have the capacity to influence others through inspiration motivated by a passion, generated by a vision, produced by a conviction, ignited by a purpose.

PART TWO:
ATTITUDES OF TRUE LEADERS

CHAPTER TEN
ATTITUDE#1
PURPOSE AND PASSION

*Man possesses the capacity to lead but
has lost the will to lead.*

The attitude of purpose is the first attribute that separates followers from leaders. **True leadership cannot be born or exist without a sense of purpose.** Purpose is the discovery of a reason for your existence and is defined as the original intent for the creation of a thing. Every human being was created for a specific purpose, and when that purpose is discovered, then a leader is born.

Purpose creates a leader because it provides an assignment for life and signals a sense of significance. You must discover your purpose and the specific contribution you were destined to make to your generation. **Your leadership is hidden in your purpose, and your purpose is the key to your passion.** No matter what position you may hold in life or in an organization, you must relate it to your sense of purpose and approach it with passion.

The attitude of passion is the second most indispensable attribute of leadership and serves as the driving

force of motivation that sustains the focus of the leader. Without passion, one lacks energy, and boredom infects one's mind and life. To become the leader that you were created to be, you must find a purpose for your life that produces a passion for living.

Every great man or woman became great because he or she possessed the spirit of passion. Yet I believe that this attitude is missing in 99 percent of the people of the world. This is why many are followers rather than leaders. Passion is rare in human experience.

PURPOSE IS THE FIRST ATTRIBUTE THAT SEPARATES FOLLOWERS FROM LEADERS.

Why is passion so important? In the Psalms, we read, "May he [God] give you the desire of your heart and make all your plans succeed." Your plans will be successful if you truly desire to accomplish them. The word *desire* denotes not a casual interest in life, but a deep, possessed drive for a desired end—a passion for a purpose. If you don't have a passion for something, you won't receive it. It's only when we have a passion for what we want to do that things start happening to enable us to fulfill it.

Every true leader is passionate. Consider the following questions: How badly do you want something? Are you just existing, or are you pursuing a reason for living? **Leaders don't just do, but they *feel* what they're doing. Their passion continually motivates and inspires them.** The average person just has a job. He puts in his time and goes home at 5:00. His work is a role he plays, not a contribution he makes to the world. **Yet true leaders don't have jobs; they have lifetime assignments.**

A COMPELLING DESTINATION FOR YOUR LIFE

Leadership is not the accomplishment of a list of goals because goals are temporary. True leadership is manifested when you discover a destination for your life that is so compelling that you will have completed your purpose for living once you accomplish it.

Passion is a key to leadership because your desire is meant to be your destiny. David, the great Israelite king, wrote in one of his psalms, "Delight yourself in the LORD and he will give you the desires of your heart." Our purposes and passions are the perpetual ideas, dreams, thoughts, and visions that fill our hearts or subconscious minds.

PASSION IS KEY TO LEADERSHIP BECAUSE YOUR DESIRE IS MEANT TO BE YOUR DESTINY.

When we delight in our relationship with our Creator, he will give us the desires that preoccupy our subconscious minds every day. This is because he has "hidden" his will inside each of us. If you want to discover God's will for your life, then look at what you desire to accomplish—the hopes and dreams that never seem to leave you. The Creator places his desires in our hearts or subconscious minds and then promises to fulfill them. Your passion is supposed to come from that hidden treasure of desire that he has put within you. You know that you have tapped into your leadership potential when you are actively involved in the things you want to do so much that you can't stop thinking about them.

Sometimes, it's not easy for us to recognize the source of our life's passion because our desires are often bigger than our pocketbooks, the level of our educations, our natural abilities, our cultures, or our race, and we figure that someone else is meant to accomplish them. Yet one of the signs of a true passion is that it is much bigger than we are. Let's look more closely at the nature of passion.

WHAT IS PASSION?

Passion may be defined as:

1. A DEEP DESIRE

   Passion is stamina that says, "I'm going to go after this, no matter what happens. If I have to wait ten years, I'm going to get it." If you want to go all the way to your dream, you can't sit back and expect everything to be easy. True leaders possess a deep desire that produces the passion to proceed with their dreams.

2. A CRAVING

   Passionate people are "possessed" people. In other words, you can't be successful as a leader unless you have a real inner need to accomplish something in particular.

3. AN OBLIGATION

   When you are passionate about something, you feel compelled to do it. **Leadership is born when one discovers a divine obligation to his community, world, and generation.**

4. A DEEP COMMITMENT

   Many people are "interested" in doing certain things, but they aren't really committed to accomplishing them. Some people say that they will get a better job, lose weight, or change their lives in other ways—some day. The world is filled with people who are merely interested, but not passionate. Commitment is the guy who jumps out of an airplane, trusting that the parachute will open. It's not talk, but action. Passion makes you jump in, no matter what. Leaders are committed, not just interested. **They are willing to put their whole selves into accomplishing their purposes. True leadership is not finding something to live for, but something to die for.**

5. A Deep Resolution

    We make New Year's resolutions every year and quickly forget them. How determined are you? Do you act on what you've committed yourself to do? Are you are willing to pay the price to obtain your desire? **True leaders are resolved in their decisions to pursue their goals and purposes.**

6. A Deep Motivation

    Passion is the juice for living. For many people, life is a drudgery. They have no motivation in regard to their jobs, spouses, education, or personal development. Someone once said that the thing about life is that it is so daily. Passion helps us to rise above our daily routines.

    If you're not motivated, then you will become a weight or burden to others. You will pull on their energy. Passion is a source of motivation. When you have passion, you don't need the right conditions to move forward because passion is internally generated and is not affected by external conditions. **True leaders do not need outside stimuli in order to take action. They are self-motivated.**

WHAT IS THE SOURCE OF PASSION?

A SENSE OF PURPOSE

Where does passion come from? First, it comes from a sense of purpose. You are pursuing something that gives your life meaning. If you become distracted or opposition stands in your way, your destiny still pulls you in the direction of your desire because you can't imagine not fulfilling it.

A SENSE OF DESTINY

Passion comes from something outside this world and is connected to it. As long as you're living for something on earth, your passion won't last. It has to be connected to something that is bigger than your own existence. If you get your passion from something on earth, then when it stops, you will stop. Yet **if you capture a sense of destiny that existed before you and will continue to exist after you, if you feel you're involved in something that is larger than yourself, then you're on your way to leadership. Passion is born when you connect to both the past and the future.**

A DEEP CONVICTION

Some people have no conviction about what they're doing, but a leader is a person of strong conviction.

Passion is a deep certainty that you need to do something. Your convictions have to do with your beliefs. If you believe that you have discovered what you're supposed to do, this creates passion. It makes you stand against and overcome opposition, resistance, criticism, and all other obstacles.

A LEADER IS A PERSON OF STRONG CONVICTION.

A REVELATION OF THE FUTURE

Passion is ignited from a revelation of where you want to go with your life. The Creator's vision for you is so vivid that you can see it in your mind's eye, and this picture creates a passion to arrive there. Most people will criticize your passion because they don't see what you see. **A leader usually moves toward things that can't yet be seen but will be manifested in the future.**

AN UNDERSTANDING OF PROVIDENCE

When you understand that the Creator's providential hand is on your life, then you know that you are not just an experiment but part of a larger program, orchestrated by God, and that you have a role to play. This causes your passion to come alive. You're not living just for yourself anymore but for all those in the past and future to whom you're tied through a common purpose. Again, **a true leader always thinks in terms of both yesterday and tomorrow—he builds *on* the past, and he builds *for* the future.**

A DEEP RESOLUTION

A person with passion is determined to accomplish what he was born to do. This is not for his own sake alone, but also for the sake of others who will be blessed through the fulfillment of his purpose.

LEADERSHIP AND PASSION

Leadership is born when purpose is discovered and destiny is understood. Passion is the driving force of leadership and energizes leadership motivation. God likes people who are passionate. In Revelation, we read of his distaste for those who are lukewarm: "I know your deeds, that you are neither cold nor hot. I wish you were either one or the other! So, because you are lukewarm—neither hot nor cold—I am about to spit you out of my mouth." People who are satisfied with a lesser existence will never go where they need to be.

In contrast, a person with passion takes chances. He is not afraid to fail because of his sense of destiny. He knows that failure is an incident but that destiny is permanent. **Leaders know that purpose is much bigger than one incident or several incidents. Instead, they keep on moving toward the fulfillment of their purposes, no matter what.**

QUALITIES OF PASSION

Leaders are those who have discovered something more important than life itself, and therefore—

- their passion produces resilience.
- their passion overcomes resistance and pain.
- their passion is a source of determination.
- their passion is an incubator of courage.
- their passion is stronger than opposition and even death.

The first-century writer Paul is a great example of a leader who was passionate. In his second letter to the church in Corinth, we find a unique passage that shows the passion he had for his vision. Some people had challenged Paul's right to be an apostle. They said that he was not really called by God and that he was not worthy of the respect he was getting. They themselves were false apostles, yet they attacked Paul's credibility and spiritual qualifications and drew people away from the truth. Paul responded by addressing the Corinthian believers who were being led astray by these false apostles. He wrote that, even if what he was about to say sounded ridiculous and foolish, he would say it anyway so that they would return to the true gospel.

LEADERS ARE THOSE WHO HAVE DISCOVERED SOMETHING MORE IMPORTANT THAN LIFE ITSELF.

Are [these other men] Hebrews? So am I. Are they Israelites? So am I. Are they Abraham's descendants? So am I. Are they servants of Christ? (I am out of my mind to talk like this.) I am more. I have worked much harder, been in prison more frequently, been flogged more severely, and been exposed to death again and again. Five times I received from the Jews the forty lashes minus one. Three times I was beaten with rods, once I was stoned, three times I was shipwrecked, I spent a night and a day in the open sea, I have been constantly on the move. I have been in danger from rivers, in danger from bandits, in danger from my own countrymen, in danger from Gentiles; in danger in the city, in danger in the country, in danger at sea; and in danger from false brothers. I have labored and toiled and have often gone without sleep; I have known hunger and thirst and have often gone without food; I have been cold and naked. Besides everything else, I face daily the pressure of my concern for all the churches.

Why did Paul give a list of problems and tribulations as part of the proof that he was a genuine apostle? He was saying, in effect, "If the vision and assignment I received wasn't real, do you think I'd go through all those hardships?"

Paul paid a price for his purpose, but his passion enabled him to do it. You are passionate and you are real if you stay steady under pressure. You know your vision is from God when you are still at it once the storm clears.

Leadership is born when one discovers his purpose for being and commits to pursue it at all costs. If you find that you are bored, then you have not yet discovered your purpose because passion is the driving force in life.

Sow a thought, reap a belief.
Sow a belief, reap an attitude,
Sow an attitude, reap an action.
Sow an action, reap a habit.
Sow a habit, reap a character.
Sow a character, reap a destiny.

CHAPTER ELEVEN
ATTITUDE #2
INITIATIVE

The greatest value you can possess is a good attitude.

T he attitude of initiative is one the most important attributes of true leaders that distinguishes them from perpetual followers. **Leaders don't wait for the future to come; they create it. They don't wait for others to do what they know they should or could do.** This is the distinction of leaders.

The inspiration of leadership is vision. A vision is a picture of what you want to accomplish. Yet the attitude of initiative makes the difference between a plan and an actual result. In other words, **vision is a desire, while initiative gets it accomplished**.

Let's look at some descriptions of initiative:

- Initiative is a catalyst.
- Initiative is taking action.
- Initiative springs from self-motivation.
- Initiators are self-starters who don't need outside urging to do something.

- Initiators make specific decisions to begin things.

The Creator is our primary example of the leadership attitude of initiative. The account of creation in the first book by Moses starts with, "In the beginning God created the heavens and the earth. Now the earth was formless and empty, darkness was over the surface of the deep, and the Spirit of God was hovering over the waters. And God said, 'Let there be light,' and there was light."

VISION IS A DESIRE; INITIATIVE GETS IT ACCOMPLISHED.

Before God spoke, the earth was formless, empty, and dark. It would have remained that way if he hadn't initiated the process of creation. He saw the potential of the earth and transformed it into something that had form, was teeming with created beings, and was filled with light. The most important lesson here is hidden in the words, "In the beginning God created." Here we see that the spirit of leadership initiates activity and activates change. This is the spirit of a leader. **Leaders don't just dream; they awaken and act on their dreams.**

THE PRINCIPLES OF INITIATIVE

1. INITIATIVE IS THE KEY TO ACCOMPLISHMENT.

There are numerous examples of inventors, composers, and others who initiated works out of their imaginations that otherwise would have remained mere potential. As you develop the attitudes of leadership, consider what ideas and desires you want to bring to reality and how taking initiative would be the catalyst for their manifestation.

2. INITIATIVE IS THE POWER OF MOMENTUM.

Merriam-Webster's 11th Collegiate Dictionary describes *inertia* as an "indisposition to motion, exertion, or change." Inertia is a fact of life. Things don't get started, progress, or get back on track once they've stalled unless someone takes action to set them on the right course again.

At a baseball game, a base coach urges on the runners to round the bases and make it to home before they are thrown out. He helps them to keep their momentum. Similarly, **the attitude of initiative enables you to be your own coach so that you maintain momentum in pursuit of your life's purpose.**

3. INITIATIVE IS THE MANIFESTATION OF DECISION.

Nothing can be accomplished unless a decision has been made concerning it. In our everyday lives, we don't buy a house, choose a dress, or select one form of insurance over another unless we specifically decide to take one thing and put aside all other options. This principle holds true as we exercise our gift of leadership. Effective leadership involves a number of decisions and choices, which can lead many people to resist and forsake procrastination. **Initiative enables us to make choices that help us to move forward in our goals.**

4. INITIATIVE IS THE KEY TO PLEASING LEADERSHIP.

Both leaders and followers appreciate the attitude of initiative in their fellow workers. When a leader is indecisive or a follower continually has to be told what to do, it is not only draining on those affected, but it is also inefficient. Leadership growth comes as a result of enthusiastically embracing and moving forward in our purposes.

INITIATIVE ENABLES US TO MOVE FORWARD IN OUR GOALS.

5. INITIATIVE IS THE MANIFESTATION OF THE SPIRIT OF CONFIDENCE AND FAITH.

We often hesitate to take initiative because we are afraid of responsibility or the consequences of our actions. The writer of Hebrews said, "But my righteous one will live by faith. And if he shrinks back, I will not be pleased with him." When we exhibit the attitude of initiative, it shows that we are operating in faith and the confidence that God will see us through as we pursue the purposes that he has for us.

6. INITIATIVE IS THE SPIRIT OF CREATIVITY.

Inventors have the habit of doing multiple experiments. They keep trying until something works. Initiative often works in a similar way. A willingness to keep starting and trying things as we pursue our purposes sparks the spirit of creativity and yields good results for those who delight in trying "one more thing."

7. INITIATIVE IS THE KEY TO OBEDIENCE.

When we know that we're supposed to do something, that is when we should begin to do it. Holding back until we feel like it or the circumstances are better is not conducive to the practice of doing what we need to do at the time that we need to do it in order to accomplish our goals.

Utilizing the Power of Initiative

How is the attitude of initiative affected by your beliefs about yourself, your purpose, and your God? Leaders utilize the power of initiative because they—

- believe in the integrity and faithfulness of their Creator.

- believe in their causes.

- believe in the rightness of their dreams.

- believe in their competence.

- are not afraid to fail.

To become the leader that you were born to be, you must cultivate the spirit of initiative. Don't wait for others to do what you know you could and should do. **Be a leader— initiate.**

CHAPTER TWELVE
ATTITUDE #3
PRIORITIES

Attitude is evidence of what you think.

All true leaders are distinguished by their strong sense of priorities. They are always clear about what is important to them and desire to attend to the principal issue at hand.

The most important thing in life and leadership is to know what you are supposed to do. Any activities that we undertake consume our time, talents, effort, energy, and life. **What we do, therefore, determines who we are and what we become. True leaders have a clear sense of what they need to do. The key to this ability is applying the principle of priority.**

WHAT IS PRIORITY?

Let's begin by defining priority. It is—

- something that has a prior claim on us.

- something that merits our primary attention.

- something that receives our primary resources.

- something that has a right to supersede other things.

239

LEADERSHIP AND PRIORITIES

Effective leadership involves the management of one's priorities. True leaders have learned how to distinguish between what is truly important for their lives and the fulfillment of their purposes and what is an urgent but temporary need. They have also discovered how to distinguish between options that are good and ones that are best for them. Because of these things, they have narrow agendas and short to-do lists.

HOW TO CHOOSE PRIORITIES

How do we determine what is really important in our lives? We find a valuable guideline in a statement by Paul in his first letter to the Corinthians: "'Everything is permissible for me'—but not everything is beneficial. 'Everything is permissible for me'—but I will not be mastered by anything."

WHAT WE DO DETERMINES WHO WE ARE AND WHAT WE BECOME.

We live in an age when, particularly in the United States and the European Union, people have a myriad of choices in regard to their lifestyles, careers, and leisure time. We can do many things, but not everything is constructive to our lives. **One of our major responsibilities as leaders is determining what is best for us according to our life's purpose and vision.**

Paul knew about being single-minded in the pursuit of a purpose. In his letter to the Philippians, he wrote,

Not that I have already obtained all this, or have already been made perfect, but I press on to take hold of that for which Christ Jesus took hold of me. Brothers, I do not consider myself yet to have taken hold of it. But one thing I do: Forgetting what is behind and straining toward what is ahead, I press on toward the goal to win the prize for which God has called me heavenward in Christ Jesus.

EVALUATE YOUR CURRENT PRIORITIES

What purposes do you need to "take hold of"—personally, professionally, and spiritually? How do your current priorities line up with them? Take time this week to think through your present priorities. Perhaps you haven't really established any priorities and are living in crisis mode: Whatever seems most pressing at the time gets your attention. Are you aware of your purpose and actively working toward it? Before setting your goals, as outlined in the following chapter, make sure that you discover your purpose and decide how to align your life and your priorities so that you will be able to fulfill your particular leadership mandate in the domain that you have been given.

THE ART OF PRIORITY IS DISTINGUISHING BETWEEN THE IMPORTANT AND THE URGENT.

To become the leader that you were created to be, you must cultivate the art of priority—choosing and distinguishing between what is important versus what is urgent. Leadership means knowing the difference between busyness and effectiveness. **True leaders make a distinction** between an opportunity and a distraction, and between what is good and what is right for them. Leaders know that priorities protect their valuable energy, time, resources, and talent.

CHAPTER THIRTEEN
ATTITUDE #4
GOAL SETTING

If you think you can do it, that's confidence;
if you do it, that's competence.

All true leaders possess a goal-driven attitude. **Leaders distinguish themselves from followers by their passion for preestablished goals.** They regulate their activities and measure their progress against prescribed objectives and milestones.

Everyone in the world is a goal setter, in one way or another. Even the man who is failing at life is setting goals that cause him to fail. In fact, many of us plan *not* to do things that would make us successful.

Many times, we don't realize that we are setting goals. Whenever we make plans to go to the grocery store, go to school, do the laundry, or meet friends for a meal, we are in reality setting goals.

When we don't achieve what we want to achieve or accomplish what we desire to accomplish, the problem is not goal setting, in itself. Instead, it's that we don't set goals for the things we truly care about, or we set the wrong kind of goals.

A leader understands how to set the right goals. This is a vital attitude to cultivate because your future and your life depend on the goals you set—either consciously or subconsciously. Where you end up in life is a result of the goals that you set or did not set for your life.

EVERYONE IS A GOAL SETTER; A LEADER
UNDERSTANDS HOW TO SET THE RIGHT GOALS.

What should determine the goals that we set and the plans that we make? Our purpose and vision in life. **Success comes from the discipline of goal setting according to one's purpose.** I have set goals for my life for the past thirty-five years, and I have goals written out for the next thirty years, because I've seen how success follows goal setting.

THE RELATIONSHIP BETWEEN PURPOSE AND PLANS

The book of Proverbs says, "Many are the plans in a man's heart, but it is the Lord's purpose that prevails." According to the wisdom of this statement, we can understand three things about the relationship between purpose and plans (goal setting):

1. Purpose is more important than plans.

2. Purpose is more powerful than plans.

3. Purpose precedes plans because the Creator established our purposes even before we were born.

We have to know and focus on our purposes before we can begin planning, because plans that don't get you to your purpose are counterproductive. Purpose is God's original intent for you. Therefore, you need to know your destination.

PROTECT YOUR GOALS

Goals protect us from the undue influence of other people. **True leaders are always zealous for and jealous of their goals because these goals represent their lives.** When our goals change, our lives change, so we must carefully guard our goals.

GOALS PROTECT US FROM THE UNDUE INFLUENCE OF OTHERS.

If you don't have any goals, other people will run your life. The great king of Israel, Solomon, declared, "Whoever has no rule over his own spirit is like a city broken down, without walls." If nothing controls and orders your life, then you are open season to other people and you won't accomplish your purpose. Remember that the more successful you become, the more people will compete for your time, so you have to guard your goals even more carefully.

Once you know your purpose, you need to understand what a goal really is.

WHAT IS A GOAL?

- A goal is an established point for achievement that leads to a greater accomplishment.

- A goal is a point of measure for progress toward an ultimate purpose.

- A goal is a prerequisite for the achievement of an ultimate plan.

THE POWER OF GOALS

Goals give us a structure for accomplishing our plans one step at a time. They give us a starting place and an ending place, and they help us to focus. Here are some of the benefits of goals:

- Goals separate achievers from dreamers.
- Goal setting is the art of discipline.
- Goals are the skeleton of the plan.
- Goals give specifics to the plan.
- Goals create targets for our energy.
- Goals protect us from procrastination.

THE PRINCIPLE OF GOALS

It is helpful to have some guidelines for the development and recording of our goals because, otherwise, we can easily lose sight of them and their relationship to our purposes:

- Goals must be defined.
- Goals must be simplified.
- Goals must be written.
- Goals must be visual.
- Goals must relate to the ultimate purpose.
- Goals must be measurable.
- Goals must be flexible.

LEADERSHIP AND GOALS

Finally, true leaders understand the nature and value of goals and how their lives are affected and influenced by them. This is why leaders have the following relationship with their goals:

- Leaders state their goals.

- Leaders communicate their goals.

- Leaders are committed to their goals.

- Leaders are regulated by goals.

- Leaders are disciplined by goals.

- Leaders stick to their goals.

- Leaders believe in their goals.

- Leaders focus on their goals.

- Leaders measure their progress and success by their goals.

- Leaders revise their goals when necessary.

- Leaders protect their goals from interference.

- Leaders transfer their goals to their coworkers and to the next generation.

If you want to be successful as a leader in your domain, make goals for your life. **The secret to leadership success is living a very focused life in line with your purpose.**

CHAPTER FOURTEEN
ATTITUDE #5
TEAMWORK

Coming together is a beginning. Keeping together is progress. Working together is success.
—Henry Ford

Trrue leaders possess the attitude of teamwork because they do not care who gets the credit. They move people from their personal and private goals to serving the needs of the common good. A team spirit manifests the difference between ambition and the pursuit of a God-given destiny: Ambition is a private thing that you want to do only for your own benefit, while destiny is a big picture that involves benefiting others.

A leader is always a team player. True leaders are always cognizant that no great accomplishment has ever been achieved by one individual. This is a practical principle, but it is also by design. Mankind was created so that people would benefit from one another's mutual contributions as they live and work together. This is so they will not become self-centered, will learn to care for the needs of others, and will be able to multiply the reach of their gifts by combining their talents as they create and produce things.

After all, God himself, though he is one unified Spirit being, expresses his creative activity through the divine teamwork of Father, Son, and Holy Spirit.

A leader understands that every person was created to fill a need. Everyone has an ability that no one else has and is indispensable in the world. Likewise, because of their unique gifts and perspectives, each human being is a solution to a certain problem that needs to be solved.

TRUE LEADERS HAVE AN ATTITUDE OF TEAMWORK; THEY DO NOT CARE WHO GETS THE CREDIT.

The attitude of being a team player is also one of a humble spirit who recognizes that he has both strengths and weaknesses and needs the strengths of others to be a support where he is weak. To become the leader that you were created to be, you must embrace and encourage the unique gifts, abilities, differences, and value that each team member brings to the whole. **Leadership success is measured by how much work one can accomplish through the team.**

PRINCIPLES OF TEAMWORK

Teamwork is defined as the ability to work together toward a common vision. Because it directs individual accomplishment toward organizational objectives, teamwork is the fuel that allows common people to attain uncommon results. Let's look at some principles of teamwork:

1. PARTNERSHIP IS THE CREATOR'S IDEA.

    When the Creator first brought mankind into the world, he had the idea of partnership in mind: "The LORD God said, 'It is not good for the man to be alone. I will make a helper suitable for him.'"

2. TEAMWORK IS NECESSARY FOR THE FULFILLMENT OF PURPOSE.

    Again, at creation, God said, "Let us make man in our image, after our likeness: and let them have dominion." The mandate of dominion over the earth, which requires the spirit of leadership, was given to both males and females. This means that teamwork is a built-in requirement for the fulfillment of our purposes in the world.

3. TEAMWORK IS THE CREATOR'S PLAN FOR LEADERSHIP.

    While God often calls individuals to carry out his purposes, he doesn't want them to pursue their callings alone. Even Moses, who was called the friend of God and did extraordinary things, needed leadership help. In the book of the prophet Micah, God said, "I sent Moses to lead you, also Aaron and Miriam." Moses did not rule alone, but was given the help of his brother and sister. At a time when Moses tried to take on too much responsibility, his father-in-law reminded him that he needed to delegate responsibility or the work would be too much for him. We also see the idea of teamwork in the first-century church with the traveling teams of Paul and Barnabus, Peter and John, and Priscilla and Aquila. When Paul worked with the churches he founded, he often had many coworkers who assisted him.

4. TEAMWORK WAS EMPHASIZED BY JESUS.

Jesus himself did not carry out his ministry alone but instead gathered a group of twelve disciples to assist him and learn from his example. When he sent out his disciples to minister, he told them to go two by two.

TEAMWORK INTRINSICALLY APPRECIATES DIVERSITY OF GIFTS.

THE BENEFITS OF TEAMWORK

Again, teamwork intrinsically appreciates the diversity of gifts that the team members bring to the partnership or group. Paul wrote, "Just as each of us has one body with many members, and these members do not all have the same function, so in Christ we who are many form one body, and each member belongs to all the others. We have different gifts, according to the grace given us." The spirit of teamwork offers the following benefits:

- Teamwork gives opportunity for participation.

- Teamwork provides the environment for people's talents and gifts to be released.

- Teamwork gives both personal and corporate satisfaction.

- Teamwork gives value to each part and member.

- Teamwork recognizes the value of each part/ person.

EFFECTIVE TEAMWORK

How can you best reflect the attitude of teamwork? Glenn Parker, in his book, *Teamwork*, offers some very helpful principles regarding keys to effective teamwork programs. Apply them to improve your leadership development:

- Start with team goals.
- Select the right people.
- Define everyone's roles.
- Empower the team.
  (Authorize the power of decision.)
- Open your talent bank.
- Appreciate style differences.
- Establish ground rules.
- Create a relaxed atmosphere.
- Prepare a work plan.
- Get the work done.
- Hold efficient meetings.
- Build external networks.
- Resolve conflicts effectively.
- Build a climate of trust.
- Communicate—and communicate!
- Get everyone committed.
- Make decisions by consensus.
- Reward team results.
- Assess team performance.
- Celebrate team accomplishments.[36]

To manifest your true leadership aptitude, you must posses the spirit of teamwork and know that, as Ken Blanchard says, "None of us is as smart as all of us."[37] Leaders know that no one can be the best at everything. But when all of us combine our talents, we can be the best at virtually anything.

> *"There is no limit to what can be accomplished if it*
> *doesn't matter who gets the credit."*
> *—Ralph Waldo Emerson*

CHAPTER FIFTEEN
ATTITUDE #6
INNOVATION

Don't resist change; contribute to it.

T he spirit of true leadership is always manifested in an innovative attitude. The very nature of leading demands an innovative spirit as leaders take followers to an as-yet undiscovered world of vision.

Innovation is the creative reserve of true leaders. The ultimate goal of leadership is to successfully achieve and accomplish a predetermined vision to fulfill a primary purpose. The role of the leader is to provide a sense of purpose, vision, motivation, momentum, and a productive environment to accomplish this task. A key quality of leadership in this regard is an innovative and creative mind-set.

THE MIND-SET OF INNOVATION

One of the principal characteristics of effective leaders is their ability to think outside the box. True leaders learn from their experiences, but they never live in them. They never live their lives by prior experiences or else they would become entrenched in the past. **Leaders don't allow the past to dictate or entrap the future.** They possess the capacity to combine old ideas and concepts in order to create new ones. They never believe that there is only one way to accomplish any task. **True leaders are never prisoners of tradition.**

OUR ABILITY TO INNOVATE COMES FROM THE FACT THAT WE ARE MADE IN THE IMAGE OF OUR CREATOR.

In light of the mind-set of the innovator, let's look at some definitions of innovation. Innovation is—

- the capacity to create new approaches and concepts to deal with old and new challenges.

- the perceptivity to see possibilities in the combination of old and new concepts.

- the creation, development, and application of untested ways of solving old and new problems.

- the capacity to think beyond the known, defy the norm, and believe in one's abilities to solve problems.

THE CREATOR'S INNOVATIVE SPIRIT

Our ability to innovate comes from the fact that we are made in the image and likeness of our Creator. The first-century writer Paul said that we are to "put on the new self, which is being renewed in knowledge in the image of its Creator." This means that the more we are transformed into the image of the One who created us, the more innovative we should be.

An examination of the attitudes and actions of the Creator's innovative Spirit leads us to the following conclusions. The Creator—

- created with diversity; he never repeated any-thing in creation.

- never did the same miracle twice in the same way.

- always solved problems in unexpected and untra-ditional ways.

- challenged humanity to think beyond its current experience.

- never believed anything was impossible.

- never dealt with humanity according to its norms and expectations.

JESUS THE INNOVATOR

One of the greatest examples of the leadership spirit of innovation is the ultimate leader, the young Jewish rabbi Jesus. During his time on earth over two thousand years ago, he demonstrated the same innovative spirit as the heavenly Father. His creativity was manifested throughout all his work among men. In performing his miracles, he never repeated any single method but always used a different approach to solve every problem.

For example, he healed the blind using several differ-ent methods. For some, he merely touched their eyes and they were made well. For another, he laid his hands on the person's eyes and put mud on them, and then laid his hands on them again to cause the person to receive his sight. For still another, he simply spoke the words, "Go, your faith has healed you," and the person was healed.

When Jesus wanted to feed thousands of people who had gathered to hear him speak, he didn't have his disciples buy food at the market, but he multiplied five loaves and two fish so that everyone was fed and had leftovers to spare.

When he raised the dead, he did so in several different ways. One time he touched a young man's coffin and then told him to get up; in another instance, he took a little girl by the hand and told her to get up; and at another time, he called out to Lazarus, who was still in his grave, and Lazarus walked out of the tomb alive. Every instance was unique and most likely tailored to the individual or to God's specific purposes at the time.

Jesus was also innovative in his methods of travel. While everyone else crossed the lake in boats, there were one or two instances in which he walked on top of the water.

Finally, one time when Jesus and his disciples needed to pay taxes and Peter was concerned about it, Jesus told him to go fishing and that the first fish he caught would have money inside its mouth that they could use to pay the taxes. His leadership style shows that true leadership demands that we always consider new ways to solve old problems.

"FORGET THE FORMER THINGS"

Having a predetermined mind-set hinders the leadership spirit of innovation. In the book of the prophet Isaiah, God said, "Forget the former things; do not dwell on the past. See, I am doing a new thing! Now it springs up; do you not perceive it?" We can apply these statements in our development as innovators.

Whenever you encounter a project, a challenge, or a problem, practice thinking in new ways and with a different mind-set. Ask the Creator to give you a fresh perspective, and see what happens! As Paul wrote, "Now to Him who is able to do exceedingly abundantly above all that we ask or think, according to the power that works in us."

To become the leader that you were born to be and to manifest the hidden spirit of leadership dormant within you, you must cultivate the spirit of innovation. Do not be afraid to rise above mediocrity. Harness creativity and explore the uncharted worlds of the untested.

DO NOT BE AFRAID TO RISE ABOVE MEDIOCRITY.

Leaders don't follow paths—they create trails. They venture where others don't dare to tread. Know that the horizon of life offers great opportunities. Leaders take time to sit and think of things that have not yet been done and then make plans to get them done. **Venture into the uncomfortable zone—innovate.**

CHAPTER SIXTEEN
ATTITUDE #7
ACCOUNTABILITY

Authority is 20 percent given and 80 percent taken.
—Peter Ueberroth[38]

The spirit of true leadership always possesses a sense of accountability and responsibility. **True leaders readily embrace submission to authority and are conscious of their stewardship of the trust given to them by those whom they serve.** The spirit of leadership seeks to be faithful to the sacred trust of the followers rather than doing what will please the leader.

In this chapter, I want to address a potential danger that leaders fall into and what we can do to prevent it. As I said earlier, the key to good leadership is the power to influence through inspiration, not manipulation. The danger of leadership is its potential for wielding power without answering to anyone else. Dictatorship and tyranny occur in the absence of a leader's submission to authority.

The protection of leadership, therefore, is in a voluntary submission to a trusted authority. The spirit of accountability is the active manifestation of submission to authority.

Accountable to Whom?

Let's begin by clarifying to whom the leader must be accountable:

1. Himself (his conscience)
2. The primary stakeholders
3. The general family of humanity
4. The Creator, as the ultimate authority

All true leaders are aware of their responsibility to higher authority. Particularly in relation to the Creator, they are aware that they are accountable before God for their words and actions.

Leaders and Accountability

A true leader is always conscious that he is not a law unto himself but should uphold established laws and treat others with respect as people made in the image and likeness of the Creator. He also listens to the advice and input of credible authority.

What Is Accountability?

In a nutshell, accountability is giving a reckoning for one's conduct and reporting on one's progress. It is also an admission of motives and reasons for taking certain actions.

The Accountable Leader

In Paul's letter to the people of Philippi, he explained that Jesus was willingly accountable to the Father when he was on earth.

ACCOUNTABILITY

Each of you should look not only to your own interests, but also to the interests of others. Your attitude should be the same as that of Christ Jesus: who, being in very nature God, did not consider equality with God something to be grasped, but made himself nothing, taking the very nature of a servant, being made in human likeness.

A TRUE LEADER IS ALWAYS CONSCIOUS THAT HE IS NOT A LAW UNTO HIMSELF.

Jesus continually referred to his accountability to the Father, making statements such as "My food...is to do the will of him who sent me and to finish his work" and acknowledging the Father's affirmation of his leadership: "The very work that the Father has given me to finish, and which I am doing, testifies that the Father has sent me." "On [the Son of Man] God the Father has placed his seal of approval." In developing the spirit of accountability, we can have no better example than his.

HOW TO BE ACCOUNTABLE

The following are some guidelines for incorporating accountability into your life:

- Commit yourself to be accountable to your personal convictions.

- Establish the Word of God as your final judge and authority.

- Appoint and submit to a group of tested, respected, credible, and mature people for advice, correction, rebuke, and instruction.

- Choose friends who are committed to the high standards of the Word of God and give them the right to judge you by it.

Perhaps the best advice for being accountable is the following, which Paul wrote to the first-century church at Colossae:

> Whatever you do, work at it with all your heart, as working for the Lord, not for men, since you know that you will receive an inheritance from the Lord as a reward. It is the Lord Christ you are serving. Anyone who does wrong will be repaid for his wrong, and there is no favoritism.

To manifest the leadership spirit hidden within you, you must embrace the attitude of accountability. Always be conscious that you are responsible to those below and above you for everything you say and do. **Be cognizant that whatever you do as a leader may be personal, but it is never totally private.** Your ultimate accountability is to the Creator of all leaders, who knows the thoughts and attitudes of your heart.

CHAPTER SEVENTEEN
ATTITUDE #8
PERSISTENCE

Change is inevitable; growth is optional.

All true leaders cultivate the attitude of persistence. **The spirit of leadership never gives up until it achieves its goal. It is a spirit that never quits.**

Nothing in the world can take the place of persistence. Talent will not—nothing is more common than unsuccessful men with talent. Genius will not—unrewarded genius is almost a proverb. Education will not—the world is filled with educated derelicts. Persistence and determination, however, are powerful forces.

Persistence is the product of faith that is generated by a purpose. It is—

- the power to hold on, in spite of everything.

- the power to endure.

- the ability to face defeat again and again and not give up.

- the knack for pushing on in the face of difficulty, knowing that victory is yours.

- taking pains to overcome every obstacle and to do what is necessary to reach your goals.

Leaders persist because they have a firm grasp of their purposes, know where they are going, and are confident that they will arrive there. Their persistence is a manifestation that they hold a conviction about their futures based on the visions they have been given for their lives. **True leaders believe that the attainment of their purposes is not optional, but that it is an obligation and a necessity, so they would never think of giving up.**

THE SPIRIT OF LEADERSHIP IS A SPIRIT THAT NEVER QUITS.

Jesus told a wonderful parable that gives us a perfect picture of persistence. It is recorded in the gospel written by Luke, the first-century physician:

> In a certain town there was a judge who neither feared God nor cared about men. And there was a widow in that town who kept coming to him with the plea, "Grant me justice against my adversary." For some time he refused. But finally he said to himself, "Even though I don't fear God or care about men, yet because this widow keeps bothering me, I will see that she gets justice, so that she won't eventually wear me out with her coming!" And the Lord said, "Listen to what the unjust judge says. And will not God bring about justice for his chosen ones, who cry out to him day and night? Will he keep putting them off? I tell you, he will see that they get justice, and quickly. However, when the Son of Man comes, will he find faith on the earth?"

This parable illustrates the power that persistence can have in accomplishing what we truly desire. At another time, Jesus told a similar parable that encourages us that success comes to those who persist—not only in the natural realm, but in the spiritual realm, as well.

> Suppose one of you has a friend, and he goes to him at midnight and says, "Friend, lend me three loaves of bread, because a friend of mine on a journey has come to me, and I have nothing to set before him." Then the one inside answers, "Don't bother me. The door is already locked, and my children are with me in bed. I can't get up and give you anything." I tell you, though he will not get up and give him the bread because he is his friend, yet because of the man's boldness he will get up and give him as much as he needs. So I say to you: Ask and it will be given to you; seek and you will find; knock and the door will be opened to you. For everyone who asks receives; he who seeks finds; and to him who knocks, the door will be opened.

As you develop the leadership spirit of persistence, remember these truths about the nature of your Creator and his own persistence in carrying out his purposes for you: (1) God is faithful; (2) God does not lie; (3) God has established his Word; (4) your purpose is already completed in him; (5) God delights in you and considers you his child.

Here are some encouraging and thought-provoking sayings about the value of persistence:

> Success seems to be largely a matter of hanging
> on after others have let go.
> —William Feather

Effort only fully releases its reward after
a person refuses to quit.
—Napoleon Hill

All great achievements require time.
—Anne Frank

Successful people keep moving. They make mistakes,
but they don't quit.
—Conrad Hilton

It's the constant and determined effort that breaks down
all resistance, sweeps away all obstacles.
—Claude M. Bristol

Success is failure turned inside out.
—Anonymous

If you have stumbled in pursuing your purpose, start again, make new plans to take the place of old ones that aren't working, and stop only when you are finished!

CHAPTER EIGHTEEN
ATTITUDE #9
DISCIPLINE

"For God did not give us a spirit of timidity, but a spirit of power, of love and of self-discipline."
—2 Timothy 1:7

O ne of the key attitudes of true leadership is that of strong self-discipline. Genuine leaders understand that self-discipline is the manifestation of the highest form of government—self-government. **The true spirit of leadership cultivates a self-control that regulates one's focus and orders one's life.** The disciplined lifestyle distinguishes leaders from followers.

WHAT IS DISCIPLINE?

Any study of the characteristics of true leaders will reveal that they all exhibit a strong self-discipline, usually motivated by a passion generated by a sense of purpose and vision. All leaders are "prisoners" of the passion of their purposes.

Discipline may be defined as self-imposed standards and restrictions motivated by a desire that is greater than the alternatives. It is a self-policing. The nature of discipline is self-management regulated by a code of conduct in keeping with a set of goals and commitments dictated by an intended result. Discipline is a series of decisions prescribed by a determined destiny.

DISCIPLINE IS A SERIES OF DECISIONS PRESCRIBED BY A DETERMINED DESTINY.

The spirit of discipline is rooted in self-control, which is a fruit of the Spirit. Leaders live with the understanding that—

- he who cannot control his thoughts will never control himself.

- he who cannot rule himself will never control life.

- he who cannot rule himself will never rule a nation.

- he who cannot control himself will be controlled by others.

DISCIPLINE LEADS TO PERSONAL TRANSFORMATION

Leaders know that the most powerful kind of control is self-control because it is the hardest to master but reaps the greatest rewards. Therefore, they are more concerned about controlling themselves than controlling other people.

According to *Merriam-Webster's 11th Collegiate Dictionary*, the words *disciple* and *discipline* come from the same root word meaning "pupil." A disciple is a student or learner who is dedicated to a concentrated and focused instruction or committed to learning to think like his or her teacher. This is why the followers of the ultimate teacher, Jesus Christ, were called his disciples, for it was his intent to take them through his "school of thought" and change their thinking so that they thought like him.

A disciple is considered an understudy, one given to or submitted to the mentoring of a master teacher. He is one who voluntarily surrenders his will to the influence of another in order to obtain the knowledge, thoughts, and philosophy of the teacher, for the purpose of personal transformation. All true leaders are students of life and for life.

VISION AND DISCIPLINE

Again, **vision is the source of the leader's discipline.** The great king Solomon's thoughts about vision are found in his book of wisdom, called Proverbs: "Where there is no vision, the people perish." Various translations of this verse give us additional insight into its meaning: "Where there is no vision, the people are unrestrained [throw off restraint]." "Where there is no revelation, the people cast off restraint [throw off self-discipline]."

VISION IS THE SOURCE OF DISCIPLINE AND THE MOTHER OF LEADERSHIP.

Vision is the source of discipline and the mother of leadership. As I said earlier, the man or woman with a clear vision lives a very focused life that requires strong self-discipline. This makes life very simple because—

1. vision chooses your future.

2. vision chooses your use of time.

3.   vision chooses your priorities.

4.   vision chooses your friends.

5.   vision chooses your reading material.

6.   vision chooses your use of energy.

7.   vision chooses your hobbies.

8.   vision chooses the movies you watch.

9.   vision chooses your diet.

10. vision chooses how you invest your money.

11. vision chooses your to-do list.

12. vision chooses your attitude toward life.

13. vision chooses your life's plan.

14. vision chooses your life.

To manifest the leadership spirit within you, you must cultivate a disciplined life and regulate your thoughts and activities based on the results that you desire for your life. The spirit of leadership is a spirit of discipline.

CHAPTER NINETEEN
ATTITUDE #10
SELF-CULTIVATION

Accept the power in self-empowerment.

T rue leaders possess the leadership attitude of self-cultivation, a passion for personal development. Some marks of a genuine spirit of leadership are a desire and commitment to gain knowledge and insights, to keep improving oneself, and to learn from others.

Leaders are consummate readers and are always looking for opportunities to advance their knowledge. They create their own learning opportunities and facilitate their own educational environments. A leader's personal collection of books is usually his greatest possession.

To become the leader that you were destined to be, you must convert your home into a university and your automobile into a mobile seminar hall. Leaders know that they must never stop expanding their knowledge base. The attitude of self-cultivation also drives them to extend their knowledge beyond their particular areas of focus in order to be versatile when necessary. Leaders study beyond the realm of their own disciplines—but in ways that will advance their purposes and visions.

As you pursue the spirit of leadership, consider the following methods of self-cultivation:

TRUE LEADERS POSSESS A PASSION FOR PERSONAL DEVELOPMENT.

- Written material: books, magazines, newspapers, journals, instructional manuals.

- Visual material: documentaries, movies, television programs, computer programs, the Internet.

- Personal contact: speakers, discussion groups, Bible study groups, professional and social organizations, counseling, friendships.

- Personal experience: the development of skills, talents, hobbies, and other areas of interest.

CHAPTER TWENTY
LEADERSHIP ATTITUDES TO CULTIVATE

You become what you think.

The subject of leadership has been studied and researched by many people throughout history. Social psychologists have, from the outset, made leadership a primary focus of their research. One of the most consistent findings by historians, sociologists, and empirically oriented social psychologists is that the nature and type of leadership exhibited depends on the particular situation, the tasks to be performed, and the unique characteristic of the leader and his subordinates.

Leaders must possess a combination of attitudes that embrace a spirit that reflects the heart and image of the Creator. Leadership is both simple and difficult because it demands an integration of the following:

1. a belief in oneself
2. a passion for one's assignment
3. a love for people
4. a willingness and capacity to walk alone
5. a sense of satisfaction from the success of others

MANIFESTING YOUR TRUE LEADERSHIP POTENTIAL

As we have discussed throughout this book, attitude is the key to the manifestation of your true leadership potential. It is defined as a mind-set based on your beliefs and convictions, and it motivates your behavior. Your attitude arises from the fundamental beliefs, convictions, and opinions that you have about yourself, your abilities, your world, and others, and it is manifested in your degree of self-confidence.

ATTITUDE IS KEY TO LEADERSHIP, AND IT MOTIVATES YOUR BEHAVIOR.

Your attitude can be transformed by the discovery of your true self-worth, your true potential, and your commitment to achieve. **The leadership attitude is more concerned with fully expressing itself than with attempting to prove itself to others.**

In addition to the ten attitudes described in this book, true leadership requires a number of other attributes that are indispensable for the effective fulfillment of vision in the twenty-first century. The following are what I call "Leadership Attitudes-to-Be," or "The Leader's 'Beattitudes.'" They describe the mind-set that every leader must embrace, cultivate, and exhibit in his or her exercise of leadership.

THE LEADER'S BEATTITUDES

1. THE SPIRIT OF RESILIENCE—the ability to see failure as temporary and a necessary step to success.

2. THE SPIRIT OF COURAGE—the ability to transform one's fear into a motivator for action and change.

3. THE SPIRIT OF PATIENCE—a belief in the potential of change and the ability to wait for it.

4. THE SPIRIT OF COMPASSION—a sensitivity to the worth of others.

5. THE SPIRIT OF SELF-VALUE—a belief in one's importance to the world.

6. THE SPIRIT OF SELF-CONFIDENCE—a trust in one's inherent abilities.

7. THE SPIRIT PERSEVERANCE—the ability never to give up or surrender to the context of a situation.

8. THE SPIRIT OF STRATEGIC THINKING—the ability to plan rather than panic.

9. THE SPIRIT OF TIME MANAGEMENT—the conscious application of time to goals.

10. THE SPIRIT OF HIGH TOLERANCE FOR DIVERSITY—a belief in the beauty and strength of variety.

11. THE SPIRIT OF SELF-COMPETITION—the practice of never comparing oneself to others but only with what one has been or done before.

Leadership is both an art and a science: It is innate and yet learned; it is inherent and yet must be developed. True leadership is the hope of the future of our world and will determine the success or failure of our homes, communities, cities, nations, and planet. If we are going to discover the true leadership potential that resides within us, we will have to consult and refer to our omnipotent Creator for the true revelation of our leadership capacity and reconnect to the true essence of our leadership assignment.

LEADERSHIP—BOTH OUR PAST AND OUR DESTINY

Leadership is truly our past and our destiny and is the only thing that will fulfill our natural passion for greatness. I challenge you to spend time with the Creator of your leadership spirit and discover the awesome joy it is to receive the power and spirit of dominion available through an intimate relationship with him. I encourage you to submit to the Authorized Dealer whom he sent to reconnect you to yourself and to his purpose and plan for your life.

YOU WERE BORN TO LEAD—SETTLE FOR NOTHING LESS.

You were born to lead—settle for nothing less. Your generation and your world await your manifestation. Do it for the unborn generations who are meant to build on the foundation of your success as a leader. Remember, the difference between a follower and a leader is attitude. We must posses the attitude of leadership. We must think, talk, walk, dress, act, respond, decide, plan, work, relate, and live like leaders. You have the leadership spirit; now you need the attitude of leadership.

We must cultivate the same attitude that eighty-five-year-old Caleb had. Forty-five years earlier, he had been one of only two men, among the ten spies sent to scout out the land, who believed that the Israelites could defeat their enemies and enter the Promised Land. When the Israelites finally did enter in and the land was being distributed, he could have chosen the easy life on the plains, but he chose the heights of the mountains. In addition, he chose the very land of the descendants of Anak, of whom the other ten spies had said, "We seemed like grasshoppers in our own eyes, and we looked the same to them." For forty years, as the Israelites wandered in the desert, Caleb's spirit of leadership was so strong that he apparently planned to take on the toughest and most fearful adversaries in the land once he had the opportunity.

Here was God's response to Caleb, and I trust that this will be his response to you after you have reread this book and begun to develop the spirit of leadership in your own life:

Because my servant Caleb has a different spirit and follows me wholeheartedly, I will bring him into the land he went to, and his descendants will inherit it.

It was his attitude that made the difference. Make it yours, too.

SERVE YOUR GIFT TO THE WORLD

To become the leader that you were born to be, you must discover who you are, your purpose in life, and the Creator's design for your existence. **Remember that a true leader learns from others but never tries to become them. You must be true to yourself.** The ingredients and essence of leadership cannot be taught. They must be discovered and learned through experience and development. This capacity to learn resides within each of us, and it is now up to us to decide whether or not we will become the leaders that the Creator intended us to be.

The point is not to strive to become a leader but to discover and become your true self. **Genuine leadership is the discovery of one's purpose and assignment for life and the inherent gift and abilities that come with that assignment. It is the commitment to serve your gift to the world in order to enhance the lives of many.**

THE ESSENCE OF LEADERSHIP CANNOT BE TAUGHT BUT MUST BE DISCOVERED.

Simply put, true leadership is serving oneself to the world. Therefore, it is not measured by how many people serve you but by how many people you serve. The spirit of leadership was defined over two thousand years ago by the most influential and effective leader of all time, a young master teacher, who, when asked how to become a great leader, responded, "Whoever wants to become great among you must be your servant,...just as the Son of Man did not come to be served, but to serve, and to give his life as a ransom for many."

APPENDICES:
MAXIMIZING YOUR LEADERSHIP POTENTIAL

ESSENTIAL QUALITIES AND CHARACTERISTICS OF TRUE LEADERSHIP

To cultivate the spirit of leadership, you must practice integrating many qualities and characteristics in your life. These are necessary attitudes for effective leadership and serve as measures of your leadership refinement as you continue to progress in maximizing your true leadership potential. All true leaders possess the following attitudes—characteristics of *the spirit of leadership*:

- ❑ **Vision**—the capacity to see beyond one's natural eyes; it is a picture of purpose.

- ❑ **Wisdom**—the capacity to apply knowledge effectively.

- ❑ **Decision making**—the ability to study consequences and make sound decisions without fear; a willingness to fail rather than avoid responsibility.

- ❑ **A positive attitude**—the ability to see people and situations in a positive way.

- ❑ **Courage**—the ability not to be controlled or paralyzed by fear; the effective management of uncertainty.

Essential Qualities and Characteristics

- **High energy**—strength and stamina to work hard and not be worn down.

- **Personal warmth**—a manner and attitude that draws people.

- **Humility**—being in touch with oneself, accepting oneself.

- **Righteous Anger**—a capacity to resist and stand against injustice and abuse.

- **Integrity**—consistency in one's words and actions; trustworthiness; true character.

- **Responsibility**—an ability to always come through; a lack of excuses; job delegated means job done.

- **A good self-image**—feeling good about self, others, and life.

- **Friendship**—the capacity to welcome and embrace others without friction.

- **Mental horsepower**—the ability to keep learning as the job expands.

- **Authority**—a highly positive influence over others.

- **Absence of personal problems**—personal, family, and business life in order.

- **People skills**—the ability to draw people to oneself and help them develop their gifts and characters.

- **Inspirational power**—the ability to communicate one's passion to others.

- **Sense of humor**—the ability to laugh at oneself and at life and to not take life too seriously.

- **Resilience**—the ability to bounce back when problems arise.

- **Track record**—experience and success in previous situations.

- **Great desire (passion)**—a hunger for growth and personal development.

- **Self-discipline**—a willingness to "pay the price" and handle success.

- **Creativity**—an ability to see solutions and fix problems.

- **Flexibility**—not afraid of change; fluid; flows with growth.

- **Sees "big picture"**—able to look beyond personal interests and see a global view.

- **Initiative**—the ability to discern what needs to be done and commence action.

- **Executive ability**—the ability to get things done; the drive to finish an assignment.

VALUES OF THE SPIRIT OF LEADERSHIP

Turue leaders have cultivated a spirit that values attributes that distinguish them from followers. If you are to manifest your true leadership abilities, you must embrace, cultivate, and value these concepts, also. I have listed them as one-word values, but you can fill in their definitions based on your own experiences and research on leadership:

- ❑ accountability
- ❑ achievement
- ❑ continuous improvement
- ❑ continuous learning
- ❑ cooperation
- ❑ courage
- ❑ courtesy
- ❑ creativity
- ❑ curiosity
- ❑ dignity
- ❑ empowerment
- ❑ fairness
- ❑ faithfulness

- ☐ generational planning
- ☐ goal orientation
- ☐ hard work
- ☐ honor
- ☐ honesty
- ☐ love
- ☐ loyalty
- ☐ no compromise
- ☐ persistence
- ☐ professionalism
- ☐ promise keeping
- ☐ punctuality
- ☐ quality
- ☐ reliability
- ☐ respect
- ☐ responsibility
- ☐ service to others
- ☐ spiritual maturity
- ☐ steadiness
- ☐ teamwork
- ☐ trust

Use this list to challenge your thinking and incorporate each concept into your daily lifestyle. Commit to applying these values to everything you do and say. Practice them in your personal life, family relationships, job, faith, school, and community life. Let your life spread the spirit of leadership throughout the world and become a carrier of the good news that everyone can become the leader that he or she was created and destined to be. Let the spirit of leadership emerge from where it has been hidden for too long.

Transforming
Followers into Leaders

Within every follower is an undiscovered leader.

The following principles are critical to your capturing the spirit of leadership for yourself and encouraging that spirit in others. All have to do with *attitude*.

- The growth and development of people is the highest calling of true leadership.

- True leaders work for the benefit of others and not for personal gain.

- The most important lesson of leadership is self-development.

- Don't ever say again, "It's too late for me to change." It is never too late to make a change.

- Not all change is improvement, but without change, there can be no improvement.

- It's not what you are that holds you back. It's what you think you are *not* that holds you back.

- The one who influences others to lead or to become leaders is a leader without limitations.

- People tend to become what the most important people in their lives think that they will become. You can literally change people's lives by your attitude and expectations of them.

- Successful people-developers make the right assumptions about people. Our assumptions will determine how successful we are in developing leadership in others.

- We can't hope for things that we're not currently working on. You will become only what you are becoming right now.

A WORD TO THE
THIRD WORLD

As the future waits, the past competes with its promises. Yet never allow the past to dictate the quality of your future. Out of the roughly seven billion people on planet earth, over four billion live in countries designated as third-world developing nations. Many of the citizens of these nations have been robbed of the opportunity and right to discover, develop, and manifest their true leadership potential due to oppressive and debilitating ideologies and systems. The greatest impact has not been the physical restrictions imposed on them, but the horrific mental damage inflicted on their self-concepts, self-worth, and self-esteem. The result is an attitude that struggles to believe that there is hope for their dreams.

What I wish to say to each third-world mind is that attitude is everything. It is more important than facts. It is more important than the past, education, money, circumstances, failures, success, and what other people think, say, or do. It is more important than appearance, giftedness, or skills. It will make or break a company, a church, or a home. The remarkable thing is that we have a choice regarding our attitude.

Attitude is the power of leadership. Nothing can stop a person from achieving success who has the right attitude.

You can always make up in attitude what you lack in education. Yet nothing can help the person who has the wrong attitude.

We cannot change the past or the fact that people will act in a certain way. We also cannot change the inevitable. But one thing we can do is to change our attitudes. Remember that your attitude is your most important asset. Invest it well and allow it to appreciate by feeding it with positive influences. Ralph Waldo Emerson said, "What lies behind us and what lies before us are tiny things compared to what lies within us."

Our attitudes cannot stop our feelings, but they can prevent our feelings from stopping us. We are responsible for our attitudes. "The pessimist complains about the wind; the optimist expects it to change; the [leader] adjusts the sail."[39] We cannot control the beauty of our faces, but we can control the expressions on them!

The future of your family, community, and nation depends on your response to the need for a new breed of leaders with a new attitude. I challenge you to report for duty and lead your generation to a better world. The children yet unborn deserve it. The key to success is this:

"Try not to become a [person] of success,
but rather try to become a [person] of value."[40]

SCRIPTURE REFERENCES

CHAPTER ONE

p. 39: "Let there be light" – Genesis 1:3.

p. 39: "Let the land produce..." – Genesis 1:24.

p. 39: "Let *us* make man..." – Genesis 1:26, emphasis added.

p. 45: As a man thinks in his heart..." – See Proverbs 23:7 (NKJV).

CHAPTER TWO

pp. 59–60: The account of Moses's life is found in the book of Exodus.

p. 60: "Land flowing with milk and honey" – Exodus 33:3 and other Scriptures.

pp. 62–63: The account of Nehemiah's life is found in the book of Nehemiah.

p. 63: "I am doing a great work..." – See Nehemiah 6:3.

pp. 63–64: The account of Queen Esther's life is found in the book of Esther.

p. 64: "Perhaps you have become queen..." – See Esther 4:14.

p. 64: "If I perish, I perish" – Esther 4:16.

pp. 65–67: The account of King David's life is found in the books of 1 and 2 Samuel, 1 Kings, and 1 Chronicles.

p. 66: "Who is this who defies...?" – See 1 Samuel 17:26.

p. 66: "Man after God's own heart" – See 1 Samuel 13:14.

pp. 72–74: The account of Paul's life is found in the book of Acts. His purpose and passion can also be seen in the letters he wrote. See the books of Romans, 1 and 2 Corinthians, Galatians, Ephesians, Philippians, Colossians, 1 and 2 Thessalonians, 1 and 2 Timothy, Titus, and Philemon.

p. 73: "Obligated both to Greeks and non-Greeks" – Romans 1:14.

p. 73: "Eager to preach to them" – See Romans 1:15.

p. 73: "I am not ashamed of the gospel" – Romans 1:16.

p. 73: The account of Paul's obstacles is found in 2 Corinthians 11:23–30.

p. 73: "constantly on the move" – 2 Corinthians 11:26.

pp. 73–74: "I have labored..." – 2 Corinthians 11:27–30.

p. 77: "A time to be born and a time to die" – Ecclesiastes 3:2.

SCRIPTURE REFERENCES

CHAPTER THREE

p. 87: "...Let the land produce vegetation" – Genesis 1:11–12.

p. 87: "...Let the water teem with living creatures..." – Genesis 1:20–22.

p. 88: "...Let the land produce living creatures..." – Genesis 1:24–25.

p. 88: "...Let us make man in our image..." – Genesis 1:26. ("have dominion": KJV).

p. 91: "Let them have dominion over..." – Genesis 1:26 (KJV).

p. 95: "Then the mother of Zebedee's sons..." – Matthew 20:20–26.

p. 96: "Instead, whoever wants to become great..." – Matthew 20:26–28.

p. 105: "I'm going to bless you... – See Genesis 12:2–3.

p. 106: "... he who gives you the ability to produce wealth" – Deuteronomy 8:18.

p. 106: "The love of money..." – 1 Timothy 6:10.

p. 106: "In that hour Jesus rejoiced" – Luke 10:21 (NKJV).

p. 107: "You can do this; come" – See Matthew 14:28–29.

p. 107: "Go ahead, do it" – See Mark 6:7–13.

p. 107: "The rulers of this world..." – See Matthew 20:25–28.

p. 108: "If anyone sets his heart..." – 1 Timothy 3:1.

p. 108: Requirements for leadership – 1 Timothy 3:2–12.

p. 109: "Let not your heart be troubled" – John 14:1–2 (NKJV).

pp. 110–111: "Angels" verses – Jude 6.

p. 111: "You will receive power" – Acts 1:8.

p. 113: "know as we are known" – See 1 Corinthians 13:12.

p. 116: "walked and talked with God..." – See Genesis 3:8.

p. 116: "Are you a king?" – See John 18:33.

p. 116: "My kingdom is not of this world" – John 18:36.

p. 117: "Father, forgive them..." – Luke 23:34.

p. 119: "Whoever does not love..." – 1 John 4:8–9.

p. 119: "If anyone says, 'I love God..." – 1 John 4:20–21.

p. 119: "'...Love the Lord your God...'" – Matthew 22:37–40.

CHAPTER FOUR

p. 126: "as a person thinks in his heart..." – See Proverbs 23:7 (NKJV).

p. 131: "Love the LORD your God..." – Deuteronomy 6:5.

p. 131: "What is the most important duty" – See Matthew 22:36.

p. 131: "Love your neighbor as yourself" – Matthew 22:39.

p. 132: "If anyone says, 'I love God...'" – 1 John 4:20.

p. 136: "For out of the overflow of the heart..." – Matthew 12:34–35.

p. 136: "But the things that come out..." – Matthew 15:18–20.

p. 136: "The good man brings good things..." – Luke 6:45.

p. 136: "every inclination of the thoughts..." – Genesis 6:5.

p. 137: "Let love and faithfulness..." – Proverbs 3:3.

p. 137: "To man belong the plans..." – Proverbs 16:1.

p. 137: "I the LORD search the heart..." – Jeremiah 17:10.

p. 137: "The word of God is living..." – Hebrews 4:12.

p. 137: "Man looks at the outward..." – 1 Samuel 16:7.

p. 138: "Where your treasure is..." – Matthew 6:21; Luke 12:34.

p. 138: "you [should] forgive your brother..." – Matthew 18:35.

p. 138: "Love the Lord your God..." – Matthew 22:37.

pp. 138–139: "...if anyone says to this mountain..." – Mark 11:23.

p. 141: "Above all else, guard your heart..." – Proverbs 4:23.

p. 141: "As water reflects a face..." – Proverbs 27:19.

p. 143: The truth will make us free – See John 8:32.

p. 144: Human beings did not retain the knowledge of God – See Romans 1:28–31.

p. 145: "light [in whom] there is no darkness" – 1 John 1:5.

p. 145: "The spirit of a man is the lamp" – Proverbs 20:27 (NKJV).

p. 146: "For You will light my lamp..." – Psalm 18:28 (NKJV).

p. 146: "No one lights a lamp..." – Luke 11:33.

CHAPTER FIVE

p. 151: "And out of the ground..." – Genesis 2:9 (KJV).

p. 151: "Let the waters bring forth..." – Genesis 1:20 (KJV).

p. 153: "Let us make man in our image..." – Genesis 1:26.

p. 153: "God created man in his own image" – Genesis 1:27.

p. 153: "The Lord God formed the man" – Genesis 2:7.

p. 153: "made [the] woman" – Genesis 2:22.

p. 154: "'Let there be light'..." – Genesis 1:3.

p. 158: "The day that you rebel..." – See Genesis 2:17.

p. 158: Adam lived for hundreds of years – See Genesis 5:5.

Chapter Six

pp. 173–174: "God presides in the great assembly..." – Psalm 82:1–8.
p. 179: "There is an evil I have seen..." – Ecclesiastes 10:5–7, 16.
p. 181: "As a man thinks in his heart..." – See Proverbs 23:7 (NKJV).
p. 182: Faith, or belief, comes by hearing... – See Romans 10:17.

Chapter Seven

p. 188: "Let them rule..." – Genesis 1:26 ("have dominion" KJV).
p. 190: "King of kings" – 1 Timothy 6:15; Revelation 17:14; Revelation 19:16.
p. 191: "In the beginning was the Word..." – John 1:1–5, 9.
p. 193: "You will know the truth..." – John 8:32.
p. 193: "I tell you the truth" – See, for example, Matthew 6:2; Mark 9:41; Luke 18:17; John 8:51.
p. 193: "I am the way and the truth..." – John 14:6.
p. 194: "In him was life..." – John 1:4.
p. 194: "The light shines..." – John 1:5.
p. 194: "The true light..." – John 1:9.
p. 195: "You will receive power..." – Acts 1:8.
p. 195: "I'm leaving to return to the Father..." – See John 14:16–18, 25–26.
p. 196: "Do not conform any longer..." – Romans 12:2.

Chapter Eight

p. 201: "Your attitude should be the same..." – Philippians 2:5.
p. 201: "Be renewed in the spirit of your mind" – Ephesians 4:23 (KJV).
p. 201: "He who has ears to hear..." – See, for example, Mark 4:9; Luke 8:8.

Chapter Nine

p. 209: "We are God's workmanship" – Ephesians 2:10.
p. 212: "The one who is in you..." – 1 John 4:4.
p. 214: "let my people go" – See, for example, Exodus 5:1.
p. 215: "be strong and courageous" – Joshua 1:6.
p. 216: "Which is the greatest commandment...?" – Matthew 22:36.
p. 216: "Love your neighbor..." – See Matthew 22:39.

CHAPTER TEN

p. 225: "May he [God] give you the desire..." – Psalm 20:4.
p. 226: "Delight yourself in the LORD..." – Psalm 37:4.
p. 231: "I know your deeds..." – Revelation 3:15–16.
p. 232: "Are [these other men] Hebrews? So am I..." – 2 Corinthians 11:22–28.

CHAPTER ELEVEN

p. 235: "In the beginning God created..." – Genesis 1:1–3.
p. 237: "But my righteous one will live..." – Hebrews 10:38.

CHAPTER TWELVE

p. 240: "'Everything is permissible..." – 1 Corinthians 6:12.
p. 241: "Not that I have already obtained..." – Philippians 3:12–14.

CHAPTER THIRTEEN

p. 244: "Many are the plans..." – Proverbs 19:21.
p. 245: "Whoever has no rule..." – Proverbs 25:28 (NKJV).

CHAPTER FOURTEEN

p. 250: "...it is not good for the man to be alone..." – Genesis 2:18.
p. 250: "Let us make man in our image..." – Genesis 1:26 (KJV).
p. 250: "I sent Moses to lead you..." – Micah 6:4.
p. 250: Moses's father-in-law counseling Moses about delegation – See Exodus 18:5–24.
p. 251: Jesus sent out his disciples two by two – See Mark 6:7; Luke 10:1.
p. 251: "Just as each of us has one body..." – Romans 12:4–6.

CHAPTER FIFTEEN

p. 255: "put on the new self..." – Colossians 3:10.
p. 256: Jesus's several methods of healing – See Matthew 9:27–30; Matthew 20:30–34; Mark 8:22–25; Mark 10:46–52.
pp. 256–257: Jesus multiplied five loaves and two fish – See, for example, Matthew 14:14–21.
p. 257: Jesus's several methods of raising the dead – See Luke 7:11–15; Mark 5:35–42; John 11:38–44.

Scripture References

p. 257: Jesus walked on the water – See Matthew 14:22–32; John 6:16–21.

p. 257: Jesus directing Peter to find money inside fish for taxes – See Matthew 17:24–27.

p. 257: "Forget the former things..." – Isaiah 43:18–19.

p. 258: "...to Him who is able to do exceedingly..." – Ephesians 3:20 (NKJV).

Chapter Sixteen

p. 261: "Each of you should look..." – Philippians 2:4–7.

p. 261: "My food...is to do the will..." – John 4:34.

p. 261: "The very work that the father..." – John 5:36.

p. 261: "On [the Son of Man] God the Father..." – John 6:27.

p. 262: "Whatever you do, work at it..." – Colossians 3:23–25.

Chapter Seventeen

p. 264: "In a certain town there was a judge..." – Luke 18:2–8.

p. 265: "Suppose one of you has a friend..." – Luke 11:5–10.

Chapter Eighteen

p. 269: "Where there is no vision..." – Proverbs 29:18 (KJV)
"...the people are unrestrained" – NASB
"...cast off restraint" – NIV, NKJV.

Chapter Twenty

pp. 276–277: For the accounts of Caleb, see Numbers 13:1–14:24; Joshua 14:6–15.

p. 277: "We seemed like grasshoppers..." – Numbers 13:33.

p. 277: "Because my servant Caleb..." – Numbers 14:24.

p. 278: "Whoever wants to become great..." – Matthew 20:26, 28.

NOTES

INTRODUCTION

[1] Joseph Guinto, "Lie, Cheat, and Steal Your Way to the Top," *American Way*, 15 July 2004, 32–35.

CHAPTER ONE

[2] <http://www.wisdomquotes.com/cat_attitude.html> (June 14, 2004)

CHAPTER TWO

[3] Francis Hesselbein, Marshall Goldsmith, Richard Beckhard, eds., *The Leader of the Future* (San Francisco: Jossey-Bass Publishers, 2000), xii.

[4] Lewis Copeland, Lawrence W. Lamm, and Stephen J. McKenna, eds., *The World's Great Speeches* (Mineola, New York: Dover Publications, Inc., 1999), 753.

[5] Winston S. Churchill, ed., *Never Give In!: The Best of Winston Churchill's Speeches* (New York: Hyperion, 2003), xxviii.

[6] *Churchill: The Life Triumphant*, Compiled by American Heritage Magazine and United Press International (American Heritage Publishing Co., Inc,), 93.

[7] *Never Give In!*, 229.

[8] *The World's Great Speeches*, 885.

[9] Roy P. Basler, ed., *Abraham Lincoln: His Speeches and Writings* (Cambridge, Massachusetts: Da Capo Press, 2001), 577–78.

[10] Ibid, 688.

[11] Ibid., 793.

[12] *The World's Great Speeches*, 864–866.

[13] <http://www.saidwhat.co.uk/quotes/m/mother_teresa_707.php> (November 22, 2004)

[14] <http://www.lucidcafe.com/library/95aug/motherteresa.html> (June 20, 2004)

[15] For a more detailed discussion of this subject, please refer to Dr. Munroe's book, *The Principles and Power of Vision* (New Kensington, Pennsylvania: Whitaker House, 2003).

NOTES

CHAPTER THREE

[16] W. E. Vine, Merril F. Unger, and William White Jr., eds., *Vine's Complete Expository Dictionary of Old and New Testament Words* (Nashville: Thomas Nelson Publishers, 1996), 244.

[17] Ibid., 136.

[18] Ibid.

[19] *Strong's Exhaustive Concordance,* #H7287.

[20] Francis Hesselbein, Marshall Goldsmith, Richard Beckhard, eds., *The Leader of the Future* (San Francisco: Jossey-Bass Publishers, 2000), xiii.

[21] *Vine's Complete Expository Dictionary,* 392.

[22] *Strong's,* #G2523.

CHAPTER FOUR

[23] David Allen, *Contemplation* (McLean, Virginia: Curtain Call Productions, 2004), 16–17.

[24] *Strong's,* #H3820 and *NASC,* #H3820.

CHAPTER FIVE

[25] W. E. Vine, Merril F. Unger, and William White Jr., eds., *Vine's Complete Expository Dictionary of Old and New Testament Words* (Nashville: Thomas Nelson Publishers, 1996), 50–51.

[26] *Strong's,* #H3335 and #H1129.

[27] *Strong's,* #H2403.

CHAPTER SIX

[28] *Strong's,* #G4102.

CHAPTER SEVEN

[29] Clifford Pinchot, "Creating Organizations with Many Leaders," in *The Leader of the Future,* eds. Francis Hesselbein, Marshall Goldsmith, Richard Beckhard, 27–28 (San Francisco: Jossey-Bass Publishers, 2000).

[30] *Strong's,* #G3056.

CHAPTER EIGHT

[31] *NASC,* #G1995.

[32] <http://www.motivational-inspirational-corner.com/getquote. html?categoryid=3> (June 14, 2004)

[33] John Maxwell, *Developing the Leader within You* <http://www. inspirationline.com/Quotes/inspirational-quotes-attitude-perception-optimism.htm> (November 7, 2004)

CHAPTER NINE

[34] <http://www.quotegarden.com/yearbook.html>

[35] Paul Meier's original quote is "Attitudes are nothing more than habits of thought, and habits can be acquired."

CHAPTER FOURTEEN

[36] Glenn Parker, *Teamwork* (Successories Library Inc., 1998), 4–40: chapter headings.

[37] <http://www.kenblanchard.com/highfive/index.cfm> (November 7, 2004)

CHAPTER SIXTEEN

[38] <http://www.time.com/time/poy2000/archive/1984.html> (February 7, 2004)

A WORD TO THE THIRD WORLD

[39] William Arthur Ward; the original wording is "...the realist adjusts the sail." <http://en.thinkexist.com/quotation/the_pessimist_complains_about_the_wind-the/227505.html> (November 18, 2004)

[40] Albert Einstein. <http://www.brainyquote.com/quotes/quotes/a/alberteins131187.html> (November 18, 2004)

ABOUT THE AUTHOR

D
r. Myles Munroe is an international motivational speaker, best-selling author, lecturer, educator, and consultant for government and business. Traveling extensively throughout the world, Dr. Munroe addresses critical issues affecting the full range of human, social, and spiritual development. The central theme of his message is the transformation of followers into leaders and the maximization of individual potential.

Dr. Munroe is founder and president of Bahamas Faith Ministries International (BFMI), an all-encompassing network of ministries headquartered in Nassau, Bahamas. He is president and chief executive officer of the International Third World Leaders Association and the International Third World Leadership Training Institute. Dr. Munroe is also the founder, executive producer, and principal host of a number of radio and television programs aired worldwide and is a contributing writer for various Bible editions, magazines, and newsletters, including *The Believer's Topical Bible, The African Cultural Heritage Topical Bible, Charisma Life Christian Magazine,* and *Ministries Today.* He has earned degrees from Oral Roberts University and the University of Tulsa, and he was awarded an honorary doctorate from Oral Roberts University, for which he is an adjunct professor of the Graduate School of Theology.

Dr. Munroe and his wife, Ruth, travel as a team and are involved in teaching seminars together. Both are leaders who minister with sensitive hearts and international vision. They are the proud parents of two children, Charisa and Myles Jr.

Power Points for Success
Bob Harrison

Let one of America's most effective motivational speakers help you improve or completely transform your life—one step at a time. In his signature enthusiastic style, Bob Harrison guides you through a variety of life's challenges, revealing how you can be an overcomer and experience increase in every area of your life. Bob's principles of increase show how to change your mind-set and build yourself up so that you can live a victorious life—physically, mentally, financially, spiritually, and relationally. Through his success strategies, Bob has positively impacted homes, businesses, and organizations around the nation and world. With *Power Points,* you can benefit from these same strategies. As you activate the truths in this book—presented in a practical and easy-to-understand manner—your life can take on dramatic new direction and power.

ISBN: 0-88368-406-3 • Hardcover • 224 pages

www.whitakerhouse.com

Secrets of Super Achievers
Philip Baker

Have you ever noticed someone who seems to have it all—a great family, financial security, and an adventurous outlook on new challenges? A great life does not happen by accident—it is chosen and requires desire, determination, and faith. Those who refuse to let life happen to them, but instead choose to make life happen, boldly break away from the security of mediocry and eagerly chase God's best for their lives. Philip Baker provides insight and direction for those seeking to be more than just average and greater than the status quo. He shows readers the secrets to perseverance, balance, focus, endurance, and courage, all with a humor and wisdom that compels and enlightens.

ISBN: 0-88368-806-9 • Hardcover • 192 pages

WHITAKER
HOUSE

www.whitakerhouse.com

deepercalling
www.deepercalling.com

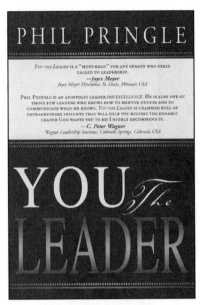

You the Leader

Phil Pringle

Do you envision future possibilities that others don't? Are you a "can-do" person? Do creative solutions to the challenges of life stir in your heart and soul? Or, have you buried these leadership characteristics deep inside because you have bought the lie that you are just a follower, not a leader? The truth is that this world is in desperate need of good, godly leaders—in other words, you and your God-given abilities. Drawing from Scripture, personal experience, and the writings of both contemporary and historical leaders, pastor Phil Pringle offers practical insights into effective leadership that can be applied in every arena of life, not just inside church walls. As you examine the attributes of dynamic leaders and the kingdom principles that govern their lives, you will discover how to realize your personal leadership potential. Explore how to implement the vision God has instilled in you—and enjoy the process of becoming the leader He has called you to be!

ISBN: 0-88368-814-X • Hardcover • 320 pages

www.whitakerhouse.com

Whether you are a businessperson, a homemaker, or a head of state, best-selling author Dr. Myles Munroe explains how you can make your dreams and hopes a living reality. Your success is not dependent on the state of the economy or what the job market is like. You do not need to be hindered by the limited perceptions of others or by a lack of resources. Discover keys to fulfilling your vision no matter who you are or where you come from. You were not meant for a mediocre life. Revive your passion for living, discover your vision, and pursue your dream.

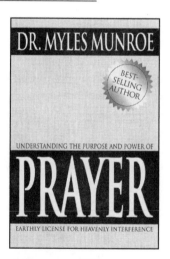

All that God is—and all that God has—may be received through prayer. Everything you need to fulfill your purpose on earth is available to you through prayer. The biblically based, time-tested principles presented here by Dr. Myles Munroe will ignite and transform the way you pray. Be prepared to enter into a new dimension of faith, a deeper revelation of God's love, and a renewed understanding that you can pray—and receive results.